Leadership
Reflections on Biblical Leadership Today

Leadership
Reflections on Biblical Leadership Today

Philip Greenslade

Copyright © 1984, 2002 Philip Greenslade.

First published 1984 by Marshall Morgan & Scott.

This revised edition published 2002 by CWR, Waverley Abbey House, Waverley Lane, Farnham, Surrey GU9 8EP.

Design and typesetting: CWR

Printed in Great Britain by Omnia Books Limited

Front cover image: © Sieger Köder, Fußwaschung. Supplied by Schwabenverlag AG.

Unless otherwise indicated, all Scripture references are from the *Holy Bible: New International Version* (NIV), copyright © 1973, 1978, 1984 by the International Bible Society. Used by permission of Hodder & Stoughton, a Division of Hodder Headline.

Other Scripture quotations are marked:

Amplified: *The Amplified Bible*, © 1987, Zondervan Corporation and the Lockman Foundation.

AV: The Authorised Version.

Barclay: William Barclay, *The New Testament. A New Translation*, Fontana/Collins, 1969.

GNB: *Good News Bible*, Collins, 1976.

JB: *The Jerusalem Bible*, Darton, Longman & Todd, 1974.

NKJV: *New King James Version*, c 1982, Thomas Nelson Inc.

Phillips: J.B. Phillips *The New Testament in Modern English*, © 1960, 1972, Fount Paperbacks.

ISBN 1-85345-202-5

To Mary

Philip Greenslade

is a respected writer and Bible teacher. He was a Baptist minister from 1969–1982, going on to serve as a staff member of the King's Church in Aldershot, England, until 1989 and he has taught at the Elim Bible College (now Regent College) in England. Philip joined CWR in 1991, developing and teaching some of our most successful programmes, including Cover to Cover Bible Discovery Weekends.

Contents

PART THREE FOLLOW MY LEADER

PART FOUR LEADERSHIP TODAY

Preface and Acknowledgments

This book made its first appearance nearly twenty years ago. Kind encouragement from friends and colleagues as to the book's continuing usefulness (and no doubt some residual authorial vanity) have prevailed over my own misgivings and led to its republication in current format. I hope to offer further reflections in forthcoming essays to be published by CWR.

This current book was written on the assumption that patterns of ministry and leadership in the Church were changing and is, therefore, still to be regarded only as a provisional statement drawn up "on the way". Its aim remains the modest one of giving clues to that biblical standard of leadership which we are all "toward" – especially perhaps for new generations of younger leaders.

What it is

Part One assumes that leadership is a good thing, asks why it is important, and suggests ways of overcoming resistance to it.

Part Two looks at how leadership emerges and functions, the difficulties it faces, the dangers it is prone to and the safeguards available to it.

Part Three looks first at the kind of leadership Jesus repudiated and then at the leadership He endorsed by His own example and teaching and bestowed as His own legacy to the Church.

Part Four surveys some of the ways in which leadership operates today and seeks to encourage the restoration of more biblical structures to the Church's life and ministry.

What it is not

Three disclaimers.

(i) It is not the literary equivalent of "painting by numbers" for leaders. This is more a "what" book than a "how-to" book.

(ii) It is not an identikit-picture of the ideal leader. Apart from the Lord

Jesus there is no such person. It is a suggestive rather than an exhaustive treatment of the theme. It reflects the period of ferment in which it was written and this needs to be taken into account. Issues that were high on the agenda in one era tend to assume a lower profile in the next. However, I trust that much of what is here touched upon has enduring value.

(iii) It is not a colouring book for leaders to be filled in with whatever shades of ecclesiastical opinion one prefers. Any readers of this book are welcome from whatever backgrounds and traditions they come, and I hope they will find it useful. Nevertheless, it still implies, as it did when first issued, the need for radical change in the wineskins the Church is currently occupying. So often, as has many times been pointed out, even the most energetic and far-seeing leaders can be crippled by obsolete institutions.

(iv) This second edition aims to be as gender inclusive as I can make it, reflecting the realities of the contemporary Church. My own tendencies and, in some cases, convictions, will be obvious to a discerning reader. But I hope that these reflections on Christian leadership will be useful to both men and women engaged in Christian ministry today. In any event, at my time of life, ideology sits less easily than it might once have done

I acknowledge now even more than I did then the unwavering support and loving help of my wife, Mary. I owe a debt of gratitude to all former colleagues in ministry, especially Derek Brown and Mike Pusey, who encouraged the original writing of the book. I continue to be immensely thankful to God for the faithful sustenance of dear friends, notably Trevor Martin and Stuart Reid, with whom these ideals have been tested in the failures and occasional successes of my own attempts to serve the Lord. I am grateful to Derek Tidball for his generous endorsement of the book second time around.

Finally, to every aspiring – or indeed, perspiring – leader, wondering where he or she fits into the picture, I offer my encouragement. As the original "square peg", I urge you not to let definition cramp your style or quench the Holy Spirit.

Philip Greenslade, October 2001

Foreword

"The writing of this book has behind it the clear desire to let God define leadership forms." So writes Philip Greenslade, revealing his goal as the author. It is a worthy ambition and one that I believe Philip has in large measure achieved.

It has become very fashionable to publish books for Christian leaders which mirror the secular leadership wisdom of the business world over which a thin veneer of Christian insight or biblical truth has been laid. Since "all truth is God's truth" there is much we can learn from such books and I have profited from many. But we must confront the uncomfortable and inescapable fact that when Jesus most directly addresses the issue of leadership He contrasts strongly the leadership style of the world and that of His own – and hence that which He expects in His disciples. He does not merely adopt and adapt what He sees around him. He radically contradicts it. "Gentile" leaders exercise authority for their own ends, set goals which are imposed in others and drive their subjects to achieve their desires. "But you are not to be like that," said Jesus. "Instead, the greatest among you should be like the youngest, and the one who rules like the one who serves."

Given this, it is right that Christian leaders should imbibe first the teaching of their Master and drink deeply at the well of Scripture before sipping the less flavoursome offerings of the contemporary world. As leaders we need discerning palates, so that we can judge the merits of secular contemporary management thinking by the wisdom of Christ and not the other way around. Philip Greenslade restores the balance and helps us to do just that.

Writing from within a charismatic and evangelical framework and firmly convinced that the Holy Spirit still gives the gifts of leadership mentioned in the New Testament letters, Philip has written a wide-ranging book, full of insight and applied wisdom. The book has the merit too of obviously having been forged on the anvil of experience. He therefore avoids the trap into which many books in this area fall: that of being good in theory but remote or even unworkable in practice. He has read widely and has a broad grasp of the issues. The short readable chapters never outstay their welcome.

Chapter after chapter yields fresh perspectives. I confess that, as with any book, there is the odd time when Philip and I might want to differ. But even on those occasions he always made me think.

From the broad initial discussion of leadership and the trawl of biblical experience, through the sharply-focused lens on Jesus and out to the broader-angled lens of images that help us to examine creatively the art of leadership in today's Church, Philip provides us with a great primer on true leadership in Christ.

I welcome this new edition of *Leadership*. Here is a book to savour. Sip it slowly. Taste it prayerfully. And however experienced a leader you are, let it enrich your ministry, correct your errors, develop your thinking and enhance your skills to the glory of the greatest leader who ever lived – Jesus.

Derek J. Tidball
Principal, London Bible College
December 2001

Part One
Why Leadership?

First Service

Jesus must be the first word in this book. He is the leader of the leaders, Lord of lords, King of kings. Before Abraham was, He was; the pioneer and perfecter of faith, a prophet eclipsing Moses, a priest superior to Aaron, David's Lord as well as son, a greater than Solomon, the Chief Shepherd of all shepherds. Going ahead of His disciples in a way that amazes and overawes us, He puts our own leadership in its proper perspective. "They were on their way up to Jerusalem, with Jesus leading the way, and the disciples were astonished, while those who followed were afraid. Again he took the Twelve aside and told them what was going to happen to him" (Mark 10:32). Clearly Jesus must have the first and last word on this subject.

"Do not be called leaders" is His starting point, a shot across the bows of this book that might have stopped it being written! Seemingly it makes for as unpromising a start to it as you could find.

Thankfully, Jesus does not leave it there but opens up our theme by adding: "For you have one teacher, the Christ. The greatest among you will be your servant" (Matt. 23:10–11). Here Jesus is not decrying leadership but redefining it. He is recasting the pattern of leadership into the shape of His own. From the outset we are reminded that any move towards leadership is a move towards the Lord Jesus Christ. "To lead is to serve." This is our basic premise, first lesson and chief ambition. We first learn to be leaders by learning to be servants. "Humility comes before honour" (Prov. 15:33).

It hardly needs saying that this is still an unfashionable note to strike in an age obsessed with celebrity, marketing and PR. No doubt the Church could do with improved efficiency. But it is definitely not where we start. Ours is a service industry not a sales industry.

Upstairs–downstairs

"Service" is a word that has long fallen on hard times. It has a rather fusty smell about it, suggestive in progressive minds of rather old-fashioned, untrendy, even illiberal attitudes. In an age where there is more talk of rights than of obligations "service" is almost regarded as demeaning. It has come to describe work that cannot be done without, but which attracts few volunteers. Everyone wants to receive it; few to give it. Usually it is assigned by default to the poor or under-privileged, to the under-educated or those with few choices. Service industries are poor relations of production industries.

In my first church as pastor, we ran a social gathering for over-60s where the senior citizens could relax in a friendly atmosphere. Often if asked, the elderly ladies would describe to me their days "in service". In those days, as young women, they served "below stairs" as chambermaids or parlour maids in the large houses of early Edwardian England. For their part, the old men, fewer in number, survivors of the Great War, still stiffened with pride as they recounted their days in the "services" as comrades in arms. "Service" even then was a concept in need of rehabilitation.

Biblically we find the concept of servanthood transformed by the prophetic vision. Isaiah dignifies for ever the idea of service in his moving prophecies of the suffering servant of God, the model for the Messiah. And when Messiah came He took the form of a servant in which to express Himself. He anticipated His coming into the world in the words of a previous servant of God: "Therefore, when Christ came into the world, he said: 'Sacrifice and offering you did not desire, but a body you prepared for me; with burnt offerings and sin offerings you were not pleased. Then I said, "Here I am – it is written about me in the scroll – I have come to do your will, O God"'" (Heb. 10:5–7 citing Psa. 40:6–8). "I am among you as one who serves." "I have come not to be ministered unto but to minister."

In radical fashion, by example and word, Jesus establishes servanthood as the way in which His followers are to lead others. He expressly repudiates every secular model of leadership in favour of servanthood. His disciples are not to be like the Pharisees, whose leadership was spoiled by hypocrisy, misuse of authority, ostentation and blatant professionalism (Matt. 23:1–7). They are not to act like Gentile rulers who "lord it over" those under them (Mark 10:32). No category, whether social, cultural, ecclesiastical or political, will fit His vision of leadership without drastic alteration in style and attitude. His "not so among you" thwarts any attempt to institutionalise worldliness in the leadership structures of His Church.

This raises a question mark against those many current leadership manuals which are weighted almost exclusively towards goal-setting, public relations techniques and management methods. Needful correctives as they are to the habitual sloppiness and inefficiency of the Church, they do not touch the mainspring of motivation in the kingdom of God.[1] As we shall see again later, it was the form of servanthood that the Son of God chose to pour His divine life into. And Father didn't break the mould when He sent Him.

For this reason the apostles never stray far from this theme in describing their own calling and that of their readers. Paul, a "bond-servant of Jesus Christ" writes to the Romans. It is as bond-servants that Peter, James, Jude and John record their testimony. The New Testament writers ransack the vocabulary of servanthood, as if to show that to be a servant is not to be a robot or automaton, but a friend and confidant and partner. Servanthood enlarges, not shrinks, our horizons. Even the original words used – *diakonos, doulos, huperetes, leitourgos* – suggest various nuances, from the servant's activity and accountability, to the authority the servant is under and the administration which is being served.

Then the whole range of words associated with *oikos* ("house") draw the commercial and domestic worlds much closer together than we are used to. In the household is where we belong with the Father and His Son. Ever since the Son and Heir came downstairs, serving has been something entirely different. And below stairs is where Jesus looks for His potential leaders. When Jesus looks for leaders He looks for those with a servant heart and a serving spirit. These servant-leaders will serve Jesus by serving His Body. "For we do not preach ourselves, but Jesus Christ as Lord, and ourselves as your servants for Jesus' sake" (2 Cor. 4:5).

Serving instructions

It is fruitful to look to the same source as the Lord Jesus for clues to this servant spirit and attitude. Psalm 40:6–8 shows us a little of what it means to be a servant. "Sacrifice and offering you did not desire, but my ears you have pierced; burnt offerings and sin offerings you did not require. Then I said, 'Here I am, I have come – it is written about me in the scroll. I desire to do your will, O my God; your law is within my heart.'"

(i) *Seek to discover what God desires not just what He requires*
The laws of sacrifice were not the total expression of God's will. God was looking beneath the offering for obedience. A true servant will look for what pleases the Lord. Our Puritan forefathers, in contrast to ourselves, rarely bothered with the problem of guidance. They merely looked each day for fresh ways of glorifying God. To have this attitude as leaders, is to begin to satisfy God's desires not just meet His requirements.

(ii) *Be wholly committed to the Lord*
The pierced ear was an ancient sign of belonging (cf. Exod. 21:1–6). Bought with a price, no believer lives an autonomous life, no spiritual leader is an entirely free agent. My leadership is not the path to emotional fulfilment for my insecure ego. I am in it for God's sake first.

(iii) *Pay attention to what the Lord is saying*
When God has got me by my ears He's got all of me! It's a poor servant who is deaf to the master's voice. Don't try to begin as a great prophet; begin as Samuel did by being awake to the smallest whisper.

(iv) *Be available!*
"Then I said: 'Here I am.'" "Here I am for you called me" is the servant spirit. Redeemed from being a slave to sin and unrighteousness, I now serve in newness of the Spirit and bring my life to attention to be of use to righteousness (Rom. 6:17–19).

(v) *Be confident about your usefulness to the Lord*
You enter the Master's presence because when called you have a right to be there. You are needed in His kingdom. You are not redundant.

You are not second reserve for the third team. Sadly there is still much unused potential in the Body of Christ because people are waiting for their name to be called or their bell to ring. What is true of them is true of their leaders, many of whom develop rapidly just as soon as someone, usually another leader, helps them to know their name and place and to identify their true gift and calling.

(v) *Do the will of God from the heart*
Once you know your destiny is written in the Book, you can embrace it with joy. Soon the Book is written into you and the law of God is etched on your heart. Duty hardly comes into it for such leaders. They delight to do the will of God. In this way fresh challenges will not deter but inspire us as leaders. If we make love our aim and earnestly desire the spiritual gifts, we will surprise ourselves by what we are able to achieve and be amazed at where we travel to as leaders in God's Church.

"You've not made much out of all these years," said an affluent merchant to an impoverished fellow Devonian who had voyaged with Drake to the New World. "Maybe not," was the reply, "but I've been with the greatest captain who's ever sailed the seas."

Full-time service

Being a servant is then deeper and greater than doing a job for God. The call to "full-time" service has nothing essentially to do with quitting one's secular work in order to study at Bible College and enter the ministry in a clerical sense. Simply by calling disciples to be in training for leadership, Jesus revises all ambitions and ruins many careers. In one of his books, that sensitive Methodist preacher of an earlier era, A.E. Whitham, muses on the possibility of there being a museum in heaven, exhibiting tokens of spiritual leadership. It's an intriguing thought. In such a museum would surely be Moses' staff and Aaron's rod – the one that budded. Alongside these, among many others, we might reasonably expect to find the inkpot that Luther threw at the devil, John Wesley's saddle and stirrups, not to mention Praying Hyde's knee patches and Billy Graham's airline tickets. But two items would surely be conspicuous by their absence. The towel and basin would not be there; for the good reason that they are still in use!

Notes

1. See the typically astringent comments by David Wells on the managerial reduction of ministry in David Wells "The D-Min-ization of the Ministry" in Os Guiness and John Seel (eds) *No God but God: Breaking with the Idols of Our Age* (Chicago: Moody Press, 1992), pp.175–188.

CHAPTER TWO

Double Fault

Nothing could be wiser for a leader, as I have discovered for myself, than to decide not to be the saviour of the world! This spares you many headaches, much heartache and not a few nervous breakdowns. As a young man with a tendency to manage other people said to E. Stanley Jones at one of the latter's retreats, "I have resigned as general manager of the universe." This is a word in season for leaders if for no other reason than that it may release us from the self-important activism that we are prone to. In the evangelical hustle and bustle of my youth, the patron saint appeared to be St Vitus and he led us an unmerry dance. The treadmill of meetings and activities, of clubs and organisations, of efforts and campaigns, seemed unstoppable. We had yet to learn that perspiration does not guarantee inspiration. We should never mistake a messianic complex for the Messianic anointing!

Stanley Jones concluded from all this that the training of leaders is too dangerous and should be left well alone, lest it produce "fussy managers of other people".[1] Jones' attack is pointed if not terminal and, in fact, helps to identify the first of two opposite errors made about leadership which I now want to look at.

Superstars

The first error made about leadership is the tendency to *over-glamorise it*. It is one of the dangers of special books about it like this one. Some leadership manuals do seem to give the impression that the ideal Christian leader can be cloned. The leader emerges as a cross between Abraham Lincoln and Napoleon; a composite of Montgomery with his meticulous preparation for battle and Patton with his daring initiatives in it. Throw in bits of the Angel Gabriel and Martin Luther King – and nowadays, Joan of Arc and Mother Teresa – and you just about have the right blend! You only have to read about Paul Yonggi Cho as you drift off to sleep and your mind goes into the fifth dimension of total fantasy. Such images of myself as a leader tend to last no longer than it takes to get up the next morning! These romantic images are, however, unwittingly reinforced by much of the admirable material published by the Church Growth School in America. Reading of the latest high-powered success story I am presented with a picture of leadership which prompts in me an unholy mixture of envy and self-condemnation. In these illustrated success stories the Senior Pastor is usually shown ensconced in managerial splendour, oozing charm and self-assurance from a deep leather swivel chair in his lavishly-appointed executive suite. Around him in the well-equipped church office are his bevy of eager colleagues. As a picture of leadership this is as impressive as it is intimidating. Rather than rejecting this image outright or rejecting ourselves in the light of it, we might do well to pull it back from a never-never land of unfulfilled dreams into the everyday world where most of us are.

In pondering the dearth of able leaders in the Church, Howard Snyder has questioned the concept of ministry implicit in the glamour view of leadership. "Is the problem really a lack of ecclesiastical superstars? Thank God for the superstars. But the Church of Jesus Christ cannot run on superstars and God never intended that it should. But he does promise to provide all necessary leadership through the gifts of the Spirit (Eph. 4:1–16)."[2] All this is good news for those churches which are open to hear what the Spirit is saying to them today. Already it is bringing release and development to whole areas of evangelicalism both inside and outside the mainline denominations. It has yet to penetrate other sections of Christendom quite different from the one we have described where an exclusive clerical monopoly still prevails. There the priest, Father, dominie or minister still stands apart or on high, on pedestal or pulpit, six feet above contradiction.

But where the Spirit has blown through our concepts of ministry to renew us in biblical principles of leadership, we have all begun to breathe again. There is a romance and a glorious dignity about true spiritual leadership to satisfy every dream, as we shall see later. But we need to approach leadership from underneath, as it were, with a healthy recognition that we are servants and that at best we make a modest contribution to the overall victory of the kingdom. The crowns and rewards are well worth waiting for.

Reverend Dogsbody

There is an opposite error to the one we have outlined which is, if anything, even more harmful to the Church. This is the tendency to *denigrate leadership*. A number of factors have contributed to this trend.

(i) There has been a decline in the status of the Christian ministry. This was especially true in Britain in the decades after the Second World War when leadership in the Church had a distinctly "fly-blown" image. The men from the ministry were all too often those wearing the hand-me-down clothes and driving the secondhand cars. This down-at-heel mentality was unwittingly reinforced by church structures which left the minister feeling like the underpaid employee of a far-from-successful business. True servanthood degenerated into servility with the minister hard pressed to maintain any legitimate sense of self-worth. Tied to a church-owned cottage or manse there was little room for manoeuvre.

Such a system was a recipe for anxiety and insecurity among Christian leaders, cramping prophetic courage. Their faithfulness exploited, pastors often seemed the doormat rather than the door to the fold. Professionalism has been the only refuge for such vulnerable people. This helps to account for the fact that ministers' fraternals often had more than their fair share of unbelief, cynicism and competitiveness. Treat someone as a hireling and you can scarcely complain if they do not prove a good shepherd. The Church gets the ministry it deserves. That this has changed or is now changing in many places is a tribute to the revolution in our thinking the Holy Spirit has inspired.

(ii) Christians have long had a love–hate relationship with leadership. Notable voices have gone on record as playing down the whole idea. "To tell a man," says Bishop Stephen Neill, "that he is called to be a leader, or that he is being trained to be a leader, is the best way of insuring his spiritual ruin, since in the Christian world ambition is more deadly than any other sin."[3] Bishop Neill was a far-sighted missionary statesman and, so, unlikely to endorse mediocrity as the pattern for the Church. But his warning reflects a double-mindedness about leadership that reaches down to every level of the Church's life. I disagree with his statement as it stands. This book would not have been attempted if I had not been sure of Paul's commitment to the truth that to aspire to leadership is to desire a "noble task" (1 Tim. 3:1).

One of the positive gains of the Church Growth movement is that we are now less shy of talking not only of success and efficiency but also of dynamic and effective leaders as needed in the Body of Christ. Here, as elsewhere, the sons of darkness have a glimmer of wisdom that the sons of light do well to notice. Throughout this book, therefore, I presuppose that leadership is a good thing, a blessed necessity, not a blessed nuisance, a gift to the Church not an imposition on it.

Double-mindedness will even confuse us here if we're not careful. Many people idolise the past and yearn for some great preacher of yesteryear to be reincarnated. Evangelicals have a pantheon of saints every bit as large as Catholics. Stirred by nostalgia, fervent saints will pray for some trumpet voice again to be raised to rally the Church and recall the world. No sooner does he arise among them saying uncomfortable things than they wish he was somewhere else altogether. Recognition has usually been posthumous. A.W. Tozer is revered "post-mortem" as a prophet by many of the very people who deny that such biblical offices are valid for today.

No one wants to return to the bad old days when the Church was a creepy mutual admiration society. Then two hours of backslapping at the Annual General Meeting was deemed adequate compensation for eleven and a half months of back-biting. Then the best thing that could be said about someone's ministry was said at their memorial service or reserved for an obituary notice. But Jesus who gave us in His ascension someone to look up to also expects us to honour and appreciate those He has delegated to represent Him. "We ask you, too, my brothers, to recognise those who work so hard among you. They are your leaders in the Lord ... hold them in respect and affection" (1 Thess. 5:12, Phillips).

(iii) The third factor I would mention as a threat to proper recognition of leadership is one which apart from this is altogether positive and welcome. That is the renewed experience of the Church as the Body of Christ in which every member has a gift to give and a role to play.

What the Holy Spirit is doing here is one of the most exciting aspects of His work today.

For this reason it would be especially tragic if this release of the potential of every member was at the expense of leadership. We do not upgrade the role of membership by downgrading the place of leaders. The priesthood of all believers is more widely practised now in churches renewed by the Holy Spirit than ever before, whatever the denominational creeds claimed. It would be wrong, however, if the priesthood of all believers was taken to mean the leadership of none. In fact, as the experience of many in leadership confirms, the release of the gifts and ministries of all the members of Christ's Body calls for more and better leadership, not less. As the gifts of the Spirit through the members express His Body, so the gifts of leadership express the headship of Jesus over it. The more prolific and varied the gifts and ministries, the more clear and respected does the leadership have to be. God's necessary order and direction, control and sensitivity is clearly to be safeguarded, not merely by liturgy or written constitution but by those at every level who have God's anointing to lead.

So we are neither superstars nor dogsbodies! Like Paul we cherish no exaggerated ideas of our own importance – "I am the least of the apostles". Like Paul we can be free of the burden of an inferiority complex – "but I laboured even more than all of them"! Like him we can rest easy in the grace of God which enables us to be just what we are and to become just what we are meant to become. Paul never minimised his calling, nor was he reticent when it came to describing it. "Paul an apostle and preacher and teacher" is his unabashed assessment. For him it was not a status symbol but rather the brand-mark of a slave. His apostleship was etched not on a brass plate outside an imposing front door but in the scars he carried and in the hearts of the saints who loved him.

He asserted his leadership when he had to for the sake of truth. He magnified his ministry in order to provoke Israel to jealousy. There is no higher dignity than to be the servant of Christ. "It is enough for the student to be like his teacher, and the servant like his master" (Matt. 10:25). Doubts about our status are dispelled when we know that our leadership is by royal appointment to the glorified Man beside the throne of God. We need not be hesitant or double-minded about what we are called to do.

After all, our service is to the right-hand court.

Notes

1. E. Stanley Jones, *The Unshakeable Kingdom and the Unchanging Christ* (Nashville: Abingdon, 1970), pp.141–142.
2. Howard Snyder, *New Wineskins* (London; Marshalls, 1977), pp.73–77.
3. Quoted by Paul Rees in *Don't Sleep through the Revolution* (Dallas: Word, 1969), p.123.

CHAPTER THREE

Undercover Agents

All servants need to be sure of their commission because sooner or later they will be asked for their credentials. "Hey! what do you think you're doing? Leave that donkey alone! Who do you think you are anyway?" One can sympathise with the owners of the animal so boldly requisitioned by Jesus. The disciples had their answer ready in advance. "If anyone asks you, 'Why are you untying it?' tell him, 'The Lord needs it' " (Luke 19:31)!

Before long the Master Himself was being asked similar questions. "By what authority are you doing these things, who gave you this authority?" It is still *the* question behind many questions. In my own early experience of a church undergoing renewal by the Holy Spirit, I discovered this to be the question at issue in whatever changes were taking place. Should we allow our tidy Baptist worship to be invaded by charismatic practices like speaking in tongues? Was it right to let people raise their hands or clap in praise to God? Should elders supplant the church meeting as the main focus of God's rule in the church? Whatever the matter in hand it became clear to me that the underlying issue was one of spiritual authority or, to put it in the terms in which it was expressed to me: "What right have you got to introduce these changes among us?"

An effective answer to this rests on a number of important considerations.

Firstly, we need to understand that spiritual leadership is part of God's kingdom rule. There has been of late a heartening rediscovery of the nature and impact of the kingdom of God. The restoration of this truth of the kingdom has been perhaps the most important feature to emerge from the contemporary charismatic renewal of the Church. There has come an appreciation of both the power of the kingdom – its dynamic aspect – and the authority of the kingdom – its governmental aspect. Some have denied one or both of these aspects. Dispensationalist writers minimise both by relegating the kingdom to the dim-distant past or projecting it into the faraway future. Charismatic dispensationalists, while affirming the power of the kingdom as operative today, postpone its governmental aspects to a coming millennium. While all our experience of the kingdom is a foretaste, a downpayment in the Holy Spirit of what is yet to come, nevertheless, what we do see now is a real representation of every aspect of the kingdom.

The same movement of the Spirit, therefore, that has brought a widespread recovery of spiritual gifts, the powers of the age to come, has at the same time brought a renewed interest in spiritual authority, the rule and order of the age to come. Our growing concern for leadership in the Church is to be seen then, I believe, as a direct consequence of our re-awakening to the kingdom dimension of our life in Christ.

One implication of this is that leadership is given, as never before, a foundation and framework which transcends all current church practice and traditions. Leaders derive spiritual authority directly from a firm commitment to this unshakable kingdom. This gives them a vision and inspiration larger than their present role or competence, bigger than their own brand of churchmanship, wider than their calling to any particular sphere or locality. The true spiritual leader is branded with the kingdom. Such a person, in the end, is the servant of no particular church and owes ultimate allegiance to no sect or denomination. With this perspective, leaders are not functionaries concerned to keep any particular institution alive; they are not propagandists for a particular party line; they are uncompromised by any special vested interest that would maintain the status quo. They can cope when every conventional view of ministry is called into question because they are dependent on none for their security.

This gives to any leader a sense of proportion and immense staying power. It means being throne-centred not man-centred. Like the psalmist, the heart is steadfast because God is exalted. Like Jeremiah, when the deceitfulness of the human heart seeks to stifle the prophetic voice, attention is directed to a glorious throne set on high. This is to know with Stephen that when earth's doors close heaven's doors open. This is apostles singing hymns in prison; this is Paul shouting "I believe God" on a sinking ship; this is Luther's "Here I stand I can do no other". This is Covenanters asserting the "crown rights of the Redeemer"; this is Corrie ten Boom confessing in Ravensbruck that there "is no pit so deep that He has not gone deeper still".

For a leader to sense a little of this is not to have illusions of grandeur. It is to embrace the indispensable romantic and heroic element in true spiritual leadership. This is kingdom iron for the soul of every leader.

The empire strikes back

The kingdom of God, then, is making such a comeback in our day that we begin to suspect it never went away. Further implications of this fact for leaders need to be spelt out.

What needs to be recognised, secondly, is that *spiritual leadership arises within the framework of God's structure of authority in His created order*. Both the business and family areas have their own appropriate pattern of authority or headship, as does the Church. "Obey your leaders and submit to their authority" (Heb. 13:17). This is no mere regression to primitive authoritarianism. In fact, as John Yoder memorably pointed out, the "household rules" enshrined in apostolic teaching (e.g. Eph. 5:21–6:9; Col. 3:18–4:1; 1 Pet. 2:13–3:7 etc) repre-sent quite revolutionary counsel.[1] These rules which show us how to "conduct ourselves in God's household" (1 Tim. 3:15) constitute what Yoder calls "revolutionary subordination". What is startling in them is that the seemingly "subordinate" partner is summoned to be a moral agent, responsible for his or her attitudes and reactions in the situation.

In this climate only the fruits of the Holy Spirit can flourish. In it the emphasis is once again on servanthood, humility and the voluntary foregoing of one's own rights. The only precedent for this is the Son's submission to His Father. He can say both "I and my Father are one" and also "My Father is greater than I". We learn from Jesus, if from no one else, that subordination is not inferiority.

Delegated authorities

Taking this further we need to state clearly a third important principle. *God directs His people and achieves consensus through delegated spiritual authorities not democratic procedures.* To say this is to run counter to the tide. But it is a vital principle to establish if God-given leadership is ever to thrive in the Church.

At once we need to counteract distortions of this view which would immediately jump to the conclusion that a dangerous authoritarianism is being advocated. Acts 6 is familiar ground for those who have walked this way of spiritual authority in recent years. What is recorded has the ring of truth for anyone attempting to put into practice what I am now describing. Luke records for us the emergence and recognition of those leaders from the Hellenistic side of the Jerusalem church who were needed to give the whole Church greater balance and maturity, and to release the apostles for wider ministry.

We find here a wonderful interaction of apostolic ministry and the people's assent. The apostles stated the need, the number and the nature of the new leaders required: the people made their choice of men with the right qualifications and brought them to the apostles for their endorsement. Here leadership is neither elected nor imposed. In the dynamic of the Spirit and in the security of godly relationships, apostolic initiatives are not blunted, nor congregational feelings overridden. This mutual recognition of what God was doing and saying about leadership brought a release to the Church that a purely democratic process would have thwarted.

This leads us to a fourth, very important principle. *To exercise spiritual authority a leader must be under authority himself.* "Your rulers are rebels" (Isa. 1:23) is the ultimate indictment of leadership as well as being a contradiction in terms.

(i) *A leader must be fully submitted to the written Word of God*
Unfortunately, this cannot be taken for granted even among those who profess to be evangelical in their view of the Bible. What is normative for doctrine or spiritual life sometimes, surprisingly, becomes relative and advisory for matters of church structure and government. Yet these

are the very areas where a leader will have to stay faithful to the Scriptures in order to lead people forward into more godly ways. As the great German scholar, Adolph Schlatter, once said, "He will not stand on the Word; he will stand under the Word."

I well remember a crucial church meeting many years ago when I and others faced a vote of confidence over the direction in which I was leading the people. Changes are seldom introduced without trouble and this was no exception. At one point a leading critic intervened in a tense debate, waving a copy of our denominational handbook. It was implied that I had forsaken the rubrics of the green book in favour of the black, leather-bound book open on the lectern in front of me! In all good faith I could only confess that I undoubtedly had and undoubtedly would continue to do just that. No doubt with the unnecessary arrogance of youth, I waved the good book back at my critic!

The fact remains that whatever the situation – in the family, in the house group, in the youth programme, in church affairs and worship – leaders have no solid ground beneath their feet except they trust implicitly in the authority of God's Word.

(ii) *A leader must be able to exercise self-control and order within the family (1 Tim. 3:1–7)*
Self-control qualifies for the exercise of control. Leaders need to be above reproach, moderate, gentle and uncontentious because they have taken themselves in hand by the power of the Spirit. "Better ... a man who controls his temper than one who takes a city" (Prov. 16:32). This is reflected in leadership in the home which is a microcosm of the Church. "For if anyone does not know how to manage his own family, how can he take care of God's church?" (1 Tim. 3:5).

Put positively, our principle makes encouraging reading. To be under spiritual authority is to have spiritual authority! Such authority is more often linked with the power of the kingdom in the Gospels. It is the authority which legitimises us to use the power of the kingdom to heal and preach and cast out demons. When a Roman centurion came to Jesus for the healing of his servant, he recognised that Jesus needed merely to speak the word for healing to take place. The explanation he gave for his confidence is very significant. " 'For I myself am a man under authority, with soldiers under me. I tell this one, "Go," and he goes; and that one, "Come," and he comes …' " (Matt. 8:5–13). As a representative of the Roman Empire, the centurion knew that he was part of a chain of command stretching back ultimately to the emperor himself. Every command he gave to a soldier or a servant in effect carried with it the authority of the emperor. His insight was to acknowledge this same principle of authority in the ministry of Jesus. Because Jesus represented His Father and was completely submissive to Him, His every word was invested with His Father's authority.

Jesus was thrilled and amazed at what this soldier was seeing by faith. For in saying "I also am a man under authority", the centurion was touching on the biblical basis for all true authority. The authority we exercise is dependent on the authority we are under. And to be under spiritual authority is to have spiritual authority.

Such credentials make room for charisma to operate. And to this we now turn.

Notes

1. John H. Yoder, *The Politics of Jesus* (Grand Rapids: Eerdmans, 1972, revd. ed 1994), p.174.

CHAPTER FOUR

Charisma

Charisma continues to be a rather fashionable commodity. Even bottles of perfume bear the word as a label. Anyone who makes a startling public impression is said to have it. But when I hear that Hitler had it and that John McEnroe had it, I'm not sure that I want it! Charisma is currently as much in vogue as servanthood and authority are not. For this reason our starting point for discovering what it really is must be elsewhere.

Biblically, it is clear that a natural personality, however colourful and impressive, is not the source of true charisma. Nor does the charisma of God's servants come from ecclesiastical training, clerical ordination, ritual or role-playing. For the servant of God charisma is a direct gift of the Holy Spirit. It comes from the Spirit's anointing or "unction" – to use the Latinised form of the word beloved of older writers. Its first impression is felt rather than understood. Charisma is that indefinable "plus" factor which gives weight to human words and force to human actions. Its absence is something we notice as much as its presence. It is not the projection of personality and yet it releases personality, investing it with power and freshness. It is an unmistakable aura which draws and holds us to some people rather than to others who may be equally eloquent or gifted. The charisma of Jesus, as James Dunn puts it, is that "mysterious ability to inspire fear and awe; confidence and trust".[1] This is the first clue in experience to the fact that the anointing of the Holy Spirit is the indispensable requirement for leaders of God's people.

Indispensable requirement

The Church is in the middle of an energy crisis. Her habitual reliance on merely natural resources is being ruthlessly exposed. As John Taylor once shrewdly said: "I have not heard recently of committee business adjourned because those present were still awaiting the arrival of the Spirit of God. I have known projects abandoned for lack of funds but not for lack of the gifts of the Spirit."[2] Thankfully times are changing. With a recognition that even the Church's natural resources are fast running out, there has come a renewed desire for the powers and resources which only the Holy Spirit can bestow. His supernatural endowment or charisma, and His spiritual gifts or charismata are now widely being seen and sought as indispensable to the Church's life and mission. We recognise now as never before that natural talents cannot build the Church; that the charisms cannot be rationalised away and equated simply with natural abilities. Accountants no longer automatically become church treasurers!

At the same time, we need to be clear that what the Holy Spirit is doing is not suppressing but releasing truly human potential. Grace does not destroy nature but redeems it. Supernatural endowments do not therefore override normal capabilities; rather they extend and enhance them. An older writer, Samuel Chadwick, put this well.

> The spirit of power sanctifies, vitalises, energises the natural faculties, and makes possible things beyond their most perfect development. The gifts of the Spirit give a supernatural power to the work of sanctified natural endowments so that men are challenged to see and consider cause and effect, and find there is nothing in natural man to account for what is manifestly of God.[3]

At the height of the charismatic renewal, Arnold Bittlinger endorsed this view by defining a charism as "a gratuitous manifestation of the Holy Spirit working in and through, but going beyond, the believer's natural ability for the common good of the people of God".[4] We might surmise that in a redeemed and restored humanity such "supernatural" abilities would be normal functions. Meanwhile, we are often still amazed by what we have said and done and achieved when under the anointing of the Holy Spirit.

The roots of this understanding of charisma are in the Old Testament. By the Spirit Bezalel was equipped to oversee the construction of the tabernacle: "… and I have filled him with the Spirit of God, with skill, ability and knowledge in all kinds of crafts" (Exod. 31:3). Judges too felt the impact of the Spirit as He prepared them for their tasks. So the Spirit "came upon" Samson (Judg. 3:10; 6:34; 14:6).

Prophets, priests and kings were consecrated for their role in a similar way, often in a dramatic ceremony involving an anointing with oil. This anointing with oil was not an empty ritual but was a true, external symbol of an internal grace. "So Samuel took the horn of oil and anointed him in the presence of his brothers, and from that day on the Spirit of the Lord came upon David in power" (1 Sam. 16:13). To David, his anointing with the Spirit was an indispensable requirement. In the wake of a self-inflicted crisis of leadership, David confesses that he can neither live nor rule without it: "Do not take your Holy Spirit from me" (Psa. 51:11).

Zerubbabel, overseeing the morale-sapping business of rebuilding Jerusalem, is reassured by personal prophecy of the presence of the anointing as the one thing needful to him: " 'Not by might nor by power, but by my Spirit,' says the Lord Almighty" (Zech. 4.6). Whether consecrated, commissioned or crowned, no leader in Israel could do without this.

Furthermore, the Spirit is the only guarantee of a living continuity. Without Him new leaders, while seeking faithfully to preserve their predecessors' position, merely perpetuate a dead tradition. Principles soon become legalism when implemented by those of lesser gift and anointing than the originators of the vision.

For this reason it is imperative that the seventy men deputed to assist Moses receive a portion of the Spirit resting on him and do not merely attempt to duplicate his methods. Moses can confidently recommend Joshua as his successor because he recognises that the younger man is "a man in whom is the spirit" (Num. 27:18). Joshua's impressive "ordination" did not bestow this anointing but only confirmed it in a public way.

When Elijah's successor Elisha received his mantle it was to set a precedent, not in clerical dress, but in desiring and needing a double portion of the prophet's spirit. Vestments are a thin disguise for the absence of an anointing which only the investiture of the Holy Spirit can give.

The charismatic Christ

A leader's need for the charisma of the Spirit is highlighted when we look at the significance of the Holy Spirit in the life of the Lord Jesus Himself. Without the Spirit the Messiah could not have lived up to His name as the Anointed One.

Accounts of His baptism and endowment with the Spirit are too full and consistent for us to minimise this. Unfortunately, for fear of adoptionist-type heresies, the Church has often underplayed the role of the Spirit in the life and ministry of the Lord Jesus. Yet it is not untrue to say that Jesus did all by the power of the Holy Spirit. He accomplished the work the Father had given Him to do not by the inherent powers of deity but by the imparted powers of deity. The eternal Son of God, incarnate, chose to fulfil His redemptive mission by the resources of the Holy Spirit in a sinless humanity. These same resources are available to us in our, as yet, far from sinless but redeemed humanity.

He was the "manifested Son" on whom the Spirit had come and remained (John 1:31ff.). He was led by the Spirit into the wilderness and full of the Spirit was sustained for forty days there until He returned to Galilee in the power of the Spirit (Luke 4:1,14). He embarked on His great "Jubilee Year" of salvation activity because, He said, "The Spirit of the Lord is upon me, because he has anointed me to preach the gospel to the poor" (Luke 4:18, NKJV). He cast out demons by the Spirit of God, bringing the freedom of the kingdom into men's lives (Matt. 12:18). He "rejoiced greatly in the Holy Spirit" as He saw the disciples sharing in the revelation of the kingdom (Luke 10:21). He was strengthened to offer Himself as a sacrifice for sin by the "eternal Spirit" (Heb. 9:14). Peter's marvellous picture of Him as the "great Itinerant" captures perfectly this charismatic dimension to the Lord's ministry. "You know ... how God anointed Jesus of Nazareth with the Holy Spirit and power, and how he went around doing good and healing all who were under the power of the devil, because God was with him" (Acts 10:38).

When we turn to our own ministry and leadership we must surely seek to be as charismatic in our measure as He was in His. Recent New Testament studies have confirmed that leadership in the Early Church was essentially charismatic not institutional. In James Dunn's words, "The authority of leadership ... was the charismatic authority of the Spirit".[5] Because leadership itself is a gift of grace from the ascended Lord by His Spirit to the Church, it immediately becomes obvious where the source of its power lies (Eph. 4:11; Rom. 12:8). The Christian leader derives authority and weight, not from any title or office, but from function, role and gift. No one is a pastor because the church noticeboard or headed writing paper says so, but because they have a shepherd heart, can feed sheep and are someone sheep will follow. As in the New Testament, true leaders cannot pull rank because they do not have any. Certainly Paul appealed to his apostolic ministry to give weight to his admonition but this was precisely an appeal to his tremendous spiritual authority, felt, in fact, as much in his absence and at a distance, as in his presence (1 Cor. 5:3ff.; 2 Cor. 13:10)!

The sixth chapter of the Acts of the Apostles shows that the fullness of the Spirit was the common factor to be looked for in emerging leaders, the one credential that could not be done without. "Choose seven men from among you who are known to be full of the Spirit and wisdom. We will turn this responsibility over to them" (Acts 6:3). Out of an overflow or surplus of faith, grace and power, a man like Stephen, full of the Spirit, ministered in a way that others found irresistible (Acts 6:5,10).

Such leaders have an abundance that makes them a source of supply to others. They are not mere deacons, but men with an already proven ministry in the Hellenistic section of the church in Jerusalem, who are now called to be elders or apostolic delegates administering a large-scale operation of pastoral care. And all this without detriment to their powerful preaching and healing ministries (Acts 6:8; 8:5ff.)! Of them it could be said, as of the elders at Ephesus, that "the Holy Spirit has made you overseers. Be shepherds of the church of God ..." (Acts 20:28).

The laying on of hands was an important feature of this release of ministry in the New Testament Church, but one which took place in a very dynamic context. To equate this with our current practice of ordination is to confuse rather than clarify the issue. Here was no formal, ritu-alised or perfunctory act of ecclesiastical machinery. Rather, in the context of prayer, those clearly recognised as apostles gave their endorsement of the Spirit's gifts and calling in others by laying their hands upon them (cf. Acts 6:6).

The strategic thrust from Antioch began in the same way (Acts 13:1–4). Here was a gathering of charismatic leaders, both prophets and teach-ers, meeting to fast and worship the Lord together. In this atmosphere the Holy Spirit spoke, presumably through prophecy, to indicate that the time was right for the setting apart of Barnabas and Saul for the work to which He had already called them. After further fasting and prayer, the laying on of hands occurred. As if to leave us in no doubt as to the source of their commission, Luke adds that the two men were "sent out by the Holy Spirit" (13:4).

Timothy, too, was "ordained" in a dynamic context with his ministry shaped and impelled by prophetic utterance and quickened by the impartation of fresh gifts. "Do not neglect your gift, which was given you through a prophetic message when the body of elders laid their hands on you" (1 Tim. 4:14 cf. 2 Tim. 1:6). "This is what is meant by charismatic leadership," says Howard Snyder, "– leadership inspired by God's Spirit, endowed with needed graces or charisms and appropri-ately recognised by the believing community."[6]

Gifts with graces

It is at this point that a worthwhile distinction can be made between the "ministries" in the Body and the "gifts" in the Body (e.g. cf. 1 Cor. 12:28 and Eph. 4:11 with 1 Cor. 12:7ff. and Rom. 12). For example, prophecy is both ministry and gift. As a ministry, prophecy is an "appointment" which all do not have (1 Cor. 12:28) whereas, as a gift, prophecy is a "manifestation" each can receive (1 Cor. 12:7). This dis-tinction is a functional not a formal one, which has to do with a person's calling, measure of faith and place in the Body. There seems to be a functional difference between a ministry gifted to enable others to serve in the Body and those gifted and enabled by it to serve the Body.

In either case we need to stress the given-ness of these abilities. It is "giving" the gift, not "possessing" the gift that is important in the kind of Body-life envisaged in 1 Corinthians 12–14, and this is as true for the leader as the led. No one can pride themselves in possessing a gift when the emphasis is on delivering the gift to others. This is as true of the gift of leadership itself. For this reason the apostolic stress is on an exhortation to "exercise the gifts", to "employ them" for the benefit of others, without thinking either too highly or too lowly of oneself (Rom. 12:3–8; 1 Pet. 4:10f.; 1 Cor. 15:10). The release and confidence this gives is priceless. Many leaders would share Howard Snyder's testimony. "When I identified and named my spiritual gifts, it seemed as if all the contradictory pieces of my life suddenly fell into place. I found the key to what God was doing in and through my life."[7]

All this is further proof of our reliance on the indispensable requirement of the Holy Spirit. Without Him we have wood without fire however "contemporary" our grasp of the principles of Body-life. Apollos is a New Testament case in point. Learning, eloquence, enthusiasm – he had everything short of the anointing. Lacking this himself he produced disciples in the same condition who expressed bewilderment when asked if they had received the Holy Spirit when they believed. Having been shown the way of Jesus more clearly, Apollos is later said to have exercised a profitable "watering" ministry in the church at Corinth (Acts 18–19; 1 Cor. 3:6). Anointed teachers water the Church: unanointed teachers merely dry out the Church. The urgent appeal made by Dr Martyn Lloyd-Jones to preachers in his great book on preaching, might well be applied to all Christian leaders: "This 'unction', this 'anointing' is the supreme thing. Seek it until you have it. Be content with nothing less."[8]

Timothy, too, is urged to stir up the gift in him in order to fulfil his ministry (2 Tim. 1:6). If the fire of the Spirit cools, Timothy will inevitably give way to his natural reticence and fail to take up his God-given responsibilities. But by kindling afresh the charisma within him, Timothy realises that he has not been given a spirit of timidity but of power and love and self-control. In short, he has been given, with the charisma, the grace needed to be a leader. By the Spirit he has the ability to dominate any situation with moral authority, to give himself in love to the brethren whatever their reaction and to maintain the necessary self-discipline that will help him keep his head in any crisis (2 Tim. 1:7). Receiving the Spirit of God in this way does not mean "that the servant of God must of necessity be a powerful personality, but that he has strength of character to be bold in the exercise of authority".[9] Timothy's example is encouraging if only because it frees us from the idea that the Spirit who indwells leaders conforms to a narrow "macho" stereotype. In fact His style is often altogether different.

Sensitivity is a mark of the Spirit. The anointed servant of God has a light touch and is not heavy-handed. The Spirit-anointed servant of God will more than likely "not shout or cry out, or raise his voice in the streets. A bruised reed he will not break, and a smouldering wick he will not snuff out" (Isa. 42:1–4). This charismatic style characterised the healing ministry of the Lord Jesus (Matt. 12:15ff.). That the root meaning of the word *"charis"* is charm is not insignificant. The English poet Laurie Lee has defined charm as a "generosity that makes no demands ... which can't withhold but spends itself willingly on young and old alike, on the poor, the ugly, the dim, the boring, on the last fat man in the corner".[10] So the Spirit will transfigure our style of leadership, opening us more to God at one end and to people at the other. Ungracious charismata are a contradiction in terms which is the point Paul is making to the Corinthians in the thirteenth chapter of his first letter.

Biblically, the root of *"charisma"* is in the *"charis"* or grace of God. New Testament leaders view their ministry as an expression and measure of this one *charis*-gift of Jesus (Eph. 4:11f.). So Paul says that from Christ he has "received grace and apostleship" (Rom. 1:5). He was made a minister, he tells us, "by the gift of God's grace given me through the working of his power" (Eph. 3:7). Paul's testimony was that the call to ministry carried with it a sense of undeserved privilege, of uncaused ability, of unusual freedom. The very grace of God in leadership bestows a sense of mastery, of spaciousness, of inner confidence and external boldness. All this is token of the fact that our leadership is carried out as servants of the new covenant, as servants of the Spirit who gives life (2 Cor. 3:6). Knowing this we can lead with an adequacy that is not of ourselves but from God (2 Cor. 3:5).[11]

Knowing that God's calling is not burdensome we can, like Timothy, stir up the Spirit's gifts within us and with gladness of heart take up the yoke of responsibility laid on us.

Notes

1. James Dunn, *Jesus and the Spirit* (London: SCM Press, 1975), p.79.
2. John Taylor, *The God-Between God* (London: SCM Press, 1972), p.5.
3. Samuel Chadwick, *The Path to Pentecost* (London: Hodder, 1932), pp.57–59, 93.
4. Arnold Bittlinger, *Gifts and Graces* (Grand Rapids: Eerdmans, 1973), p.18.
5. James Dunn, *Jesus and the Spirit* op. cit. pp.176–182.
6. Howard Snyder, *The Community of the King* (Downers Grove; IVP, 1977), p.84.
7. Howard Snyder, *New Wineskins* (London: Marshalls, 1977), p.128. A useful chart which helps to identify one's gifts has been designed by Selwyn Hughes and is available from CWR.
8. D.M. Lloyd-Jones, *Preaching and Preachers* (London: Hodder & Stoughton, 1971), p.328.
9. D. Guthrie, *The Pastoral Epistles*, Tyndale Commentaries (London: The Tyndale Press, 1964), p.127.
10. Laurie Lee, *I Can't Stay Long* (Middlesex: Penguin, 1978), p.70.
11. I hope to offer more recent reflections on this in my next book, forthcoming from CWR.

CHAPTER FIVE

Where the Buck Stops

"Taking responsibility" sounds altogether more prosaic than "exercising leadership" and it is. Responsibility does not come in glossy packaging and therefore has few immediate takers. I am reminded of the classic story of the police recruit given an interesting scenario for his initiative test. Called to the scene, he arrives to be jostled by a panic-stricken, nearly incoherent man and to find a crowd gathered round two other men clearly intent on killing each other. Behind them a burglar is obviously breaking into the house of one of the spectators. The panic-stricken man has by now managed to get through to him that his wife is about to give birth to a baby, that the ambulance men are on strike and that his own car has broken down! The recruit has hardly taken this in before he notices that across the street a fire is rapidly spreading through a block of flats and a woman is shouting for help from a top-floor window! Asked what to do in such a situation the confused recruit is alleged to have written: "Take off uniform and merge with the crowd."

At some time every leader, I suspect, would like to do just that. Under the pressure of conflicting demands, in the confusion of competing priorities, every leader has been tempted to opt out of all responsibilities. So the phone always rings on your much needed day-off when you've promised to take the children out or when you've just started that extra-special, intimate, dinner-for-two with your spouse. Blessed are you if you can answer the phone without impatience or leave it off the hook without guilt.

In fact, in the current renewal of the Church, it's very difficult to take off your uniform and merge with the crowd. The reason for this is not, as might once have been true, that the leader cannot afford to let his mask of professionalism slip for a moment – though sadly for some this may still be the case. Nor is it to say that a leader can never relax, be off-duty, or "unstring the bow".

Thankfully, and not before time, we are all learning that God-given discipline of rest and recreation which keeps our humanity in good shape. What makes it well-nigh impossible to take off one's uniform to merge with the crowd is precisely the nature of life in the Body of Christ. Having taught the people of God that each has a God-given role, gift and function to contribute to the Body, the leader finds it harder to be the exception to the rule. We cannot shed our uniform of ministry and gift in order to merge with them because they're all in uniform anyway! Nothing looks sillier or indeed more conspicuous than a leader misguidedly attempting to recede into the background. It is false pride to claim the best seat at the feast as Jesus made clear. It must surely be false modesty however for a man with the gift of leadership to take the back seat!

I recall the unease I felt when I tried to tried to sit in the back row of our worship meetings, as a sense of disquiet rose within me. This I found was not, as I first thought, a sign of pride, but clear evidence that I was meant to be a leader. I could not skulk in the background for whatever high and holy motives without denying my gifts and calling in God. No one called to be a front person can sit easy in the back row. "The buck stops here" was how Harry S. Truman felt from behind his presidential desk. And where the buck stops is where leadership begins. The heart of a true spiritual leader is a readiness to accept God-given responsibility to "take charge".[1] For anyone called to be a leader this is as much an instinct as a duty and certainly not a burden to be discarded. For all the pains and pressures of his apostolic calling, Paul showed no inclination to join Apostles Anonymous.

Abdication crisis

People of my parents' generation still recall the day in 1936 when in a poignant radio broadcast to an awe-struck nation, the King of England announced his abdication from the throne. For love of Mrs Simpson, Edward VIII passed up his crown. It's not hard to feel sympathy for him. Equally it is not difficult to conclude as you read the story of the sad later years of increasing ignominy, self-indulgence and wasted potential, that here was a man who saved his common life but lost his kingly soul.

This is an apt parable of the human plight, the root cause of which is our failure to take responsibility. Since original sin shows up more clearly in leadership than anywhere else, the leader needs to know more than anyone the roots and *raison d'être* in the grace and calling that are more original than sin. There is much to be said for the view that in Genesis 3 man's original sin is not pride but *sloth*. Leaving it to one's spouse or to the snake is our great Adamic mistake. Our rebellion is less an aggressive coup d'état, more a passive abdication, a stubborn refusal to rise to our royal calling. Our tragedy is not that we usurp a throne but that we settle for less than our kingly destiny. What the Mediaevals called "accidie", the sin of withdrawing into passivity, is really our chief temptation and the one most to be blamed for the dearth of spiritual leadership in the family and in the Church. Resignation is more dangerous than over-ambition in a leader, who is more likely, however busy, to die of boredom than over-exertion.

William Booth's famous statement that "all my best men are women" is not to be taken as a prescient endorsement of some radical feminist ideology but as an indictment in its time of male apathy. Brave and incredibly heroic women saints once outnumbered men on the mission field because men failed to rise to the challenge of their calling. Strong women, it used to be said, were the bane of the Church. They are not. Weak men are the bane of the Church. Weak kings who abdicate in favour of divorced socialites have their parallel in the history of God's people. Even the most prophetic leader at times of self-pity and defeatism can, like Elijah, want to withdraw from ministry under the oppression of the spirit of Jezebel that still stalks the Church.

"Dominion-havers"

Our training of leaders to take responsibility in the kingdom of God has its roots in Genesis 1 and is a recognition of our renewal by the Holy Spirit into the image of God (cf. Col. 3:1–25). In Leonard Verduin's inelegant but telling phrase, every human being is meant to be a "dominion-haver". We are called to share in God's rule as His co-regents. [2] We are invited by grace to reproduce our kind, peopling the earth with obedient children, walking with God. We are called to replenish the earth, to fill up its lack, to add to life not merely subtract from it. We are further commissioned to restore the earth by subduing it, bringing it back under its original rule to its true order and arrangement. This is where spiritual leadership takes its rise. Our prospectus for leadership comes from the creation order not the careers' office. This is why to aspire to leadership is to desire a "noble task" (1 Tim. 3:1).

Realising this, a leader can resist the temptation to pass up the responsibilities and settle for an easy life. When the house-group lapses into deadly silence and no one knows what to do or say, it is the house-group leader who has to make a move – even if the decision is that there is no more to be said! In doing so the cell-leader will, on a small and homely scale, be exercising dominion. "To exercise dominion in the given situation is to fasten one's will upon that situation."[3] Insignificant as it seems the leader has found the lever that lifts a world. On the basis of redemption and in the renewal of the Holy Spirit we can break out from the paralysing effects of original sloth.

This freedom obliges us of course to be much more open and honest in our confession of weakness. Original sloth puts up a clever smoke-screen to mask its work; it's called "rationalisation". This tendency to explain away is one of sin's deepest scars. Every insurance company has a long litany on file of excuses people have made for accidents they have been responsible for.

"I collided with a stationary truck coming the other way."

"The guy was all over the road. I had to swerve a number of times before I hit him."

"I had been driving for 40 years when I fell asleep at the wheel and had an accident."

"My car was legally parked as it backed into the other vehicle."

"The pedestrian had no idea which direction to run, so I ran over him."

"But they all alike began to make excuses" was how Jesus pictured the invited guests in his parable as they tried to evade the responsibility of deciding for or against His kingdom. Refusing to make excuses, a Christian leader today can face squarely the situations which call for the fastening of the will upon them.

Withdrawal symptoms

"And grant me a willing spirit, to sustain me" (Psa. 51:12) is a prayer of a leader when feeling the pressure to withdraw. The opposite of a willing spirit is a withholding spirit and it shows up in many different situations faced by a leader. "I have had enough, I can't be bothered" is how it talks. Sometimes this is the direct result of sin, as in Psalm 51. Often it is the consequence of overwork, tiredness and strain.

We may find ourselves *withholding in worship*. Listless and heavy, we find it hard to lift up our hearts. We let others do it whose emotional resources seem more adequate. This may be the time for various moods to be expressed in the body of Christ. More often than not it reveals a refusal to pay the price of worship, to make the sacrifice of praise. Worship is first explicitly mentioned in the Bible in connection with the supreme offering of Abraham, who gained God's favour, as God told him, "because you did not withhold your only son".

Withholding in the ministry of the Word is a temptation that comes to every preacher. Dogged by criticism or fear or tedium, we may hold back as we give the Word. We check our spirits so that though the words go out we don't give of ourselves in speaking them. They go out without power or passion because we are not putting our heart into them.

In the same way that Peter "began to withdraw" (Gal. 2:12) from the Gentiles, so may we tire in pressing through with relationships. Maybe we fear being misunderstood or being hurt again, or what others might think. Whatever the reason a subtle cooling off of our affections takes place. We begin to "stand aloof" *withholding in relationships*. We need especially as leaders to replenish our emotional reservoirs if we are not to succumb to this spirit. Once our affections become regularly restrained worse dangers befall us. "We have spoken freely to you,

Corinthians, and opened wide our hearts to you. We are not with-holding our affection from you, but you are withholding yours from us" (cf. 2 Cor. 6:11–12). Even the stimulus to action is lost. "If anyone has material possessions and sees his brother in need but has no pity on him, how can the love of God be in him?" (1 John 3:17). *Withholding in good deeds* may be the start of a process of decline that ends with hypocrisy and satanic deception (cf. Acts 5:3). A heart which is at the secret source of every precious thing can be different. "One man gives freely, yet gains even more; another withholds unduly, but comes to poverty" (Prov. 11:24).

So this pressure to withhold is another symptom of the original sloth and the points where it arises are danger points for leaders. "Watch the things you shrug your shoulders over" was Oswald Chambers' word of wisdom. This is the Sargasso sea of leadership where we become becalmed, unwilling to begin things, or finish things or face things. The sluggishness of the sluggard paralyses us. And the proverbial slug-gard is usually an ordinary mortal who, in Derek Kidner's words, "has made too many excuses, too many refusals and too many postpone-ments. It has all been as imperceptible and pleasant as falling asleep."[4]

Response ability

Alert to the danger of failing to take up our God-given responsibilities, we can be reassured as leaders about the built-in safeguards of doing so. God does not make impossible demands upon us, nor impose unrealistic responsibilities beyond our capacity to bear. His commands bring His enablings, as the old adage goes.

Leaders who know the safeguards are less likely to take on more than they can cope with. They will have a realistic estimate of themselves. "For by the grace given me I say to every one of you: Do not think of yourself more highly than you ought, but rather think of yourself with sober judgment, in accordance with the measure of faith God has given you" (Rom. 12:3). Knowing our measure of faith we will know too when the moment has come to increase our faith and venture into ground never taken before. But we will not over-reach ourselves. Although we will have cause to return to this point later, it is right to make it here. For a leader needs to know that to be called to bear others' burdens (Gk. *"baros"*) is not to be required to share their unique load (Gk. *"phortion"*) of responsibility (Gal. 6:2,5). "What shall this man do?" is not always my concern. "Mind your own business" is liable to be the Lord's reply!

Instead, leaders are given with their calling, special gifts of the Holy Spirit. These give them the ability to respond to the grace of God that can equip them for their tasks. Filled with the Holy Spirit, a leader can take responsibility without being overwhelmed by it. If you have the gift of leadership you know you can "exercise it with enthusiasm" (Rom. 12:8, William Barclay's translation). As a Spirit-filled leader you can be told to "exert yourself to lead" (NEB). Stimulated and strengthened by God the Holy Spirit you can react with zest to the responsibilities of leadership. Sustained with a willing spirit, you will not grow weary in well-doing. Even though you are a "conscript" you will still be able to maintain the enthusiasm of a volunteer. If you as a leader refuse to pass the buck, those you lead will imitate you and will become a responsive and responsible people.

Notes

1. Elizabeth Elliot, *The Mark of a Man* (London: Hodder & Stoughton, 1981), pp.77ff.
2. See Leonard Verduin, *Somewhat Less than God* (Grand Rapids: Eerdmans, 1970), chapter two.
3. Ibid. p.28.
4. Derek Kidner, *Proverbs*, Tyndale Commentaries (London: The Tyndale Press, 1964), p.43.

Part Two
Looking at Leadership

The Music and the Call

Great music is a great inspiration. It can take us out of ourselves and, strangely, at the same time deeper into ourselves. Music, in P.T. Forsyth's words, "opens the fountains of a greater deep and bathes us in a world of victory".[1] So it was with Isaiah. Caught up in heaven's worship, he is made conscious of heights in God and depths in himself previously unknown to him. In this experience he finds the call to his life's work.

His heart leaps to a melody that soars above the plainsong of sinners. His heart beats to the eternal rhythm of a higher order than time. He finds himself lifted above earth's discords into the ultimate harmony of heaven. He realises, in contrast, how out of step he is, how out of tune the world is, how offbeat its response, how sullen its song and radical its rebellion. Awe-struck, he is summoned to share in the ministry of reconciliation this realisation demands. Ruined and restored, cleansed and claimed, he becomes a chosen instrument of God.

This is heady stuff but is not so far a cry as it may seem from visiting the widows and caring for the fatherless. Isaiah is touching the One who works for good in everything with those who love Him. He is absorbing the scale of the symphony and, in doing so, is making sense of all the parts of which it is made up, including His own.

The Composer

There is then an *ultimate* calling; what might be described as the *call of the Father*. It is a call to serve God first of all in His big world not my little one! This stops me at once being a big fish in a small pond. The Father's call, like a tidal wave, submerges my pettiness and sweeps me out into larger seas. From fishing for fish in the local lake, Christ's disciples are called to fish for people in the ocean of the world. This is the call to share the Father's heart, to feel what He feels, to identify with His interests, to be committed to what He is committed to, to see with His eyes. To look at leadership with this wide-angle lens is vital in order to set it in its true perspective. Looked at this way, my service for God takes on a new grandeur and dignity. A veteran missionary to China is said to have been asked to take up a post with a large business firm. Well-qualified by his knowledge of the country's language and culture, he was certain to be well-paid for his work. When each successive salary offer was refused, the exasperated business man asked the missionary how much it would take to secure his services. "Oh," said the missionary, "your first offer was more than enough. The salary is fine but your job is too small!"

A sense of our ultimate calling not only gives scale to our leadership but also security. A call from God to be a leader is the mere outcrop of a very big rock. "Before I formed you in the womb, I knew you" (Jer. 1:5) gives Jeremiah the timid prophet great confidence. Paul finds his security in being an apostle not in any human decision but in Him "who set me apart from birth and called me by his grace" (Gal. 1:15). This is what it means to know the call of the Father. It is to realise that the call of God to serve Him in ministry only highlights the mysterious election that has long preceded it. What makes you a minister of God is part of what makes you a child of God in the first place. Knowing where our leadership stems from should in turn help us to see where the credit is to go. From Him by grace alone; back to Him in glory and praise. This is the order of things for leaders. Many famous composers have in fact been plagiarists. In their finest masterpieces we can detect a snatch of someone else's melody, or a variation on someone else's theme. So it is with us as leaders. No one gets the credit but the original composer. Whenever I lose my way, the call of the Father, like the call of the sea, draws me back. Deep calls to deep, usually in worship, and the clarity of my calling comes home afresh.

The Great Conductor

It is an amazing privilege that this ultimate call becomes an intensely *personal* call. The Father's claim on my life comes home to me as the *call of the Son*. He calls me by name. And Jesus only calls those He wants. "Jesus went up on a mountainside and called to him those he wanted" (Mark 3:13). Leaders truly called of God enjoy the privilege and satisfaction of being wanted. They neither volunteered for this, nor were they pressganged into it as if anyone would do for the job. Here we move in the realm of friendship rather than recruitment. Jesus wants me; He wants my heart, He wants my company. He wants me to come in close to Him before I go out from Him. Communion comes before commission. "He appointed twelve ... that they might be with him" (Mark 3:14). Any ministry I may have is born and nourished in fellowship with Him.

Here, too, I find myself alongside fellow-workers. I discover that the call of God is the call to serve the Son of God in the fellowship of His Body. There is really no place for the freelance ministries that strew the scene in today's Church. Our calling is in the context of "one body" (Col. 3:15) and our ministry is meant to be an expression of it. I am part of an orchestra responding to the Conductor. If at any time I play a more prominent role it is not without the backing and support of the other players. It is a concerto but not a sonata. The ministries of Ephesians chapter 4, prominent as they seem, are nonetheless "for the body", meant to equip others to play their part and know their place. A leader's personal relationship with Jesus is the key to personal fulfilment here. We take our timing from Him too. If the tempo slackens we do not lose heart for there are slow movements in the work. If we have to wait for recognition we can be patient for He will cue us in at the right time.

The Spirit of the piece

Most of our minor failures in leadership are due to inattention to detail, lack of concentration, moodiness and day-dreaming on the one hand; and impulsiveness and presumption on the other. This does not make you a total failure as a leader, for, as P.T. Forsyth put it, "Beethoven was not troubled when a performer struck a wrong note, but he was angry when he failed with the spirit of the piece". So it is with a leader's God. Even when our hearts condemn us He is greater than our hearts and He knows that we love Him (1 John 3:20; John 21:17). "The final judgement is not whether we have at every moment stood, but whether having done all we stand."[2]

Our calling can further be described as the particular *calling of the*

Spirit. We are called as leaders to serve God the Holy Spirit in the flexibility and variety of His ways. The Holy Spirit pinpoints the call of God for us. "This not that" is what you are to do; "here not there" is where you are to go; "now not then" is when you are to do it. Because the Spirit is interested in the small-scale things I find greater joy in attending to details; I concentrate more even in the dull moments so as not to miss His presence. He lights up my moodiness by His freshness and jolts me out of day-dreaming to find Christ in the immediate need before me. He stills my over-eagerness and calms my fevered brow. He puts colour into the drabness of ordinary days. He puts variety into the sameness of my work. Filled with the Spirit I do not treat everyone who comes to me in the same way. I give up stock answers and learn to wait for His words of wisdom. I begin to discover unexpected delights in mundane events. Even in the slow movements or when waiting my cue I find I am humming the tune and am gripped by the spirit of the piece.

His ways are all the more interesting for being so elusive. Peter knew the call of the Father and had heard the commission of the Son but it took the Spirit to bring him, dazed with his own bravado, to the house of Cornelius. What the Spirit showed him in a vision pushed back the walls of Peter's closed mind, exposing him to startling new possibilities. He had only one defence for his action – "The Spirit told me to have no hesitation about going with them" (Acts 11:12).

Again, the Spirit articulates what till then has been a felt but unspoken call of God. "The Holy Spirit said: 'Set apart for me Barnabas and Saul for the work to which I have called them' " (Acts 13:2). Ordination, over which so much controversy still rages, is simply our recognition of the gifts and calling made manifest by the Spirit in another person. "So after they had fasted and prayed, they placed their hands on them and sent them off" (Acts 13:3).

The Spirit makes specific what is only general. He focuses the overall call of God on the particular point of need. So going into all the world to preach the gospel, the apostolic team is prevented from entering Bithynia and diverted by vision to Macedonia (Acts 16:6ff.) where God is already at work laying the basis of their success. The Spirit's dazzling variety of gifts, ministries and effects gives scope for every leader to find a place and to function with great joy. We need not envy others or compete with them. We can fulfil our calling however minor because we are being filled and fired by the spirit of the piece.

Chosen instruments

What the call of God can do to a person is graphically illustrated in the life of Abraham. Its first effect is *obedience*.

(i) "By faith Abraham, when called, obeyed" (Heb. 11:8). There is no alternative when God calls. The old advice to those thinking of entering the full-time ministry "if you can do anything else do it" had this understanding of the call of God behind it. Leaders who know their calling confess to a certain constraint on their life. Necessity is laid on them and frees them from further choice.

(ii) The call issues in *movement*. Obeying the call, Abraham "went out" (Heb. 11:8). Taking off his slippers, he put on his walking shoes again. The call of God often uproots us, raises many eyebrows, ruins many a career. It leaves fishing businesses managerless and hangs "situations vacant" signs in tax-office windows.

(iii) God's call engages us with a great adventure story. Abraham went out "*though he did not know where he was going*" (Heb. 11:8). A call which is too well-defined too soon is suspect. The call of God is open-ended, unconditional, trading on our trust. "The life of Jesus," said F.B. Meyer, "was planless." Not aimless of course but planless; He relied on hearing what the Father was saying and working where He was working at every turn of the road. "It has cost the writer much to find his way so far. And he has yet a long way to go. But he believes he has found the true and magnetic North. And a voice is in his ears."[3] Obedience is a mobile home, you can park it anywhere.

(iv) All this implies *progress and change*. Those called to be leaders find themselves caught up in a "momentum apart from themselves", to use D.T. Niles' words. This keeps us going. We feel ourselves to be part of a great continuity of leaders of God's people. "As I said to

David ... as I was with Moses so I will be with you" – become personal reassurances to us of our ability to be of use and to rise to the next challenge. The "upward call of God" fascinates and attracts us and we press on eager to see the face behind the voice.

(v) The goal of this calling is an *inheritance* (Heb. 11:8). Leadership of God's people has uncertain prospects as a career but ultimate rewards as a vocation. Moses disdained the riches of Egypt because he was looking to the reward. Abraham owned not one inch of the promised land but owning nothing he possessed all things. For this is a heavenly calling (Heb. 3:1) whose rewards lie beyond carnal horizons.

Watching a nun dressing the revolting wounds of a leper, a traveller said: "I wouldn't do that for 10,000 dollars." "I wouldn't either," was her reply.[4] The call of God will make us enigmas, strangers and exiles on the earth like our fathers in the faith.

We can take heart in facing the challenges of this by remembering that the "gifts and calling of God are without repentance". Entranced by the Piper at the Gates of Dawn, Rat turns to his friend Mole.

"It's gone," sighed Rat. "So beautiful and strange and new! Since it was to end so soon, I almost wish I had never heard it. For it has roused a longing in me that is pain, and nothing seems worthwhile but just to hear that sound once more and go on listening to it for ever. No! There it is again! Now it passes on and I begin to lose it," he said presently. "O Mole! The beauty of it! The merry bubble and joy, the thin, clear, happy call of the distant piping! Such music I never dreamed of, and the call in it is stronger than even the music is sweet! Row on Mole, row! *For the music and the call must be for us.*"[5]

Notes

1. P.T. Forsyth, *Christ on Parnassus* (London: Independent Press, 1959), p.225.
2. P.T. Forsyth, *God the Holy Father* (London: Independent Press, 1957), p.110.
3. P.T. Forsyth, *Positive Preaching and the Modern Mind* (London: Independent Press, 1967), p.vii.
4. Quoted by James Stewart in *The Wind of the Spirit* (London: Hodder, 1968), pp.43–44.
5. Kenneth Graham, *The Wind in the Willows* (London: Methuen, 1936), p.92.

CHAPTER SEVEN

The Vision and the Dream

Revelation is vital to leadership. God's view of things not ours has been the starting point for all great movements of God in history. It is not enough to have a call from God. We need to know who God is, and where He wants to take His people. "I have a dream" has set things off in God's direction from Joseph to Martin Luther King. And "not disobedient to the heavenly vision" has been the resolve of all those determined to see things through once they have begun. Once having glimpsed the glory of God's plan and purpose, God's chosen instrument can stir and motivate the people of God, keeping them on course when the going gets rough as it usually does. It was long after I had studied First Corinthians in the original Greek that the vision of the Body of Christ with its varied gifts and functions dawned on me by spiritual revelation. I felt as if I had never read the New Testament before. The eyes of my heart were opened to new truth which fired my heart and shaped my ambitions in leading God's people.

To miss this is to court disaster. For "where there is no vision, the people perish" (Prov. 29:18, AV). The "vision" which this much quoted text speaks of, is to be taken in its exact sense of the revelation a prophet receives. This gives a rendering: "Where there is no *prophetic vision [among the leaders]* the people whom they lead become confused, disorganised and rebellious."

To say "I have no clear vision for this church" is the saddest thing any pastor can say. Without revelation, today's leaders can easily succumb to ungodly pressures from both inside and outside the Church. From within is the pressure which says "We want more of this" or "We must cater for that". From the outside comes the pressure of principles from the latest bestseller, or trends from the latest Bible-week and conference. It is tempting in today's Church to be an opportunist – adopting ideas simply because they are fashionable or endorsed by prominent figures in the evangelical or charismatic sub-culture. This is not to deny that pressure is often good for us nor, of course, that God speaks to us through others. But if we are to avoid the fatal trap of legalism we cannot afford slavishly to copy others. We need leaders who by the Spirit's revelation of truth to their own hearts *have seen for themselves* the purpose of the living God. Borrowed ideas and techniques will make us feel as overwhelmed and as heavy-footed as David in Saul's armour.

This ought not to deter us from having big visions. A British ambassador in Washington was once asked by a television reporter sometime before the event what he would like for Christmas. Modestly, courting no favours or inducements, he declined to say. When pressed he eventually said he would be happy with a small box of crystallised fruit. Months later on Christmas Eve the programme came on screen. The French ambassador, when asked what he would like for Christmas, said that he would like peace in the world and new agreements between nations; the German Ambassador said he wanted a new upsurge in international trade; the British Ambassador that he would like a small box of crystallised fruit! Beware your small ambitions!

The ministry of glory

A revelation of God Himself is the first essential for a leader. "The God of glory," we are told, "appeared to our father Abraham" (Acts 7:1). And in some measure this has been true for all who have significantly affected the lives of God's people.

Jonathan Edwards talks of a day in 1737 when walking in the woods he had a view that was extraordinary "of the glory of the Son of God as Mediator between God and man, and his wonderful, great, full, pure and sweet grace and love". Men as diverse as Howell Harris, Charles Finney and D.L. Moody all tell of similar experiences. "I can only say," wrote Moody, "that God revealed Himself to me and I had to ask Him to stay His hand."[1] That such experiences have often been associated with the sealing or baptism in the Holy Spirit is not surprising since it is to the ministry of the Spirit which is with glory that we are called (2 Cor. 3:8). Such initiations into visions of glory make us susceptible thereafter to more frequent revelations and insight, which go on clarifying our call and ministry. What is happening here is that in revelation the call of God breaks the surface of our consciousness in a new way. By revealing Himself to us God takes up the option on our lives His prior grace has given Him. "But when God, who set me apart from birth and called me by his grace, was pleased to reveal his Son in me so that I might preach him among the Gentiles ..." (Gal. 1:15–16). Paul's own testimony burned into my heart as a very young man. Subsequent revelations of God to me by His Spirit have served only to illustrate the prior call of God on my life, making me secure in what I am doing and enlarging the vision of what I want to become.

From the bush burning with the glory of God yet unconsumed, Moses was given a revelation of God and His purposes for Israel that shaped the future of both leader and people.

Where there is vision

The effect on a people of a leader with revelation can be seen in Moses' leadership of Israel which had the promised land in its sights (Exod. 3:8).

(i) *A leader with a clear vision gives to God's people a true sense of their destiny*
Lifted above their own pre-occupation with themselves, God's followers rejoice in being part of God's larger plans and purposes in the earth. Leaders with vision bring to the people a true taste of God's glory. This glory becomes their chief end. No longer is it a kingdom of man with God to serve in it but a kingdom of God with men to serve in it. Not only do we rejoice that we have been taken out of our "Egypt" but that "Egypt" is being taken out of us. Without a revelation of God's glory and purpose we may rest in the knowledge that God is "for us" but never venture on the fact that "we exist for God".

(ii) *A visionary leader brings coherence to God's people*
This vision holds them together, unites their disparate energies and gifts, channels their diverse abilities into one common good. Without a prophetic vision from its leaders a company of people fragment, each person going off at his own tangent, following his own guidance. Lacking this unifying objective, people become "unrestrained" or

"scattered" (Prov. 29:18). That "everyone did as he saw fit" (Judg. 21:25) in the days of the Judges could be traced directly to the fact that "in those days the word of the Lord was rare; there were not many visions" (1 Sam. 3:1). Eventually, lacking a unifying sense of purpose, the people become disorganised and ungovernable.

(iii) *The vision that a leader brings to God's people breeds endurance in them*

The Lord used a prophet to bring Israel up from Egypt and "by a prophet he cared for him" (Hosea 12:13). Like its leader, Israel "endured as seeing Him who is invisible". The leader with vision can keep people going and keep them on course. Without knowing at every phase exactly where we're going we can know what we're heading for! This spares us from many diversions and cul-de-sacs. A leader with a clear vision from God of what God wants His people to become will be able to prise them away from the merry-go-round of incessant activity and turn them in God's direction. When I first entered the Baptist ministry I was amazed to find how many organisations were kept going long after losing any inspiration they might once have had from God. No one ever questioned whether God wanted us to run this organisation again the next year. "As it was in the beginning, now, and ever shall be", seemed to be the motto. The "anniversary" disease confirmed this cyclic view of how things went. Every year the same special events turned up with such monotonous regularity that the sense of pointlessness was reinforced in our minds. The leader with vision gets the people out of this rut of going round and round the same mountain and points them to the unknown future with its promise of glory and fighting to be achieved.

(iv) *A leader with vision provides continuity for the people*

Because such leaders attract people to their vision and not just to their personality, the way is open for worthy successors to whom has been transmitted the same dreams. Fired as Moses had been with the vision of the promised land, Joshua did not head up a "Threshold of Canaan Church" which settled where Moses had stopped. He had the Spirit of Moses and so led the people on into the land Moses had seen with the eyes of his heart right from the beginning. Rather than stop where I stop I would rather you started again from where I started.

The price of the vision

"Keep paying the price of the vision. Let God see that you are willing to live up to the vision."[2] To see what this can mean we turn again to the life of Abraham.

(i) *Vision makes me willing to live in "tents"* (Heb. 11:9–10)
Because he was "looking for a city" Abraham was willing to live in a tent even *in* the promised land! In other words the price that has to be paid for the vision is willingness to live in transition. It is to preface every ministry with a "towards". This means accepting that we inhabit the interim, where every extrabiblical definition is preliminary, every prophecy is partial, every arrival a new starting-point. The cost of vision is felt in every seeming failure when what we experience falls short of what we envisage. The great "not-yet" of a salvation that is to come wipes the smirk of satisfaction off the face of the complacent, the critical and the apathetic. Equally it wipes the smile of smugness off the face of a naive and false triumphalism. Only the sight of the city enables you to live in the tent without disillusionment. Those who refuse to pay the price of the vision become either idealists or cynical reactionaries.

(ii) *Vision will cost me friendship*
The vision that draws me to those whose hearts burn with the same glow, will cut me off from others whose blood runs cold at the thought of the unknown. Many who set out together in recent years in the adventure of the Spirit have parted company because where one was taken on the other was left, hugging his caution. In any great movement of God there are those swept along by the tide, who do not have the call of the sea in them; those who climb onto the bandwagon but do not have the tune ringing in their hearts. There are those for whom the revelations coming from the Holy Spirit today have become merely interesting topics for discussion rather than convictions they would die for.

So Abraham has to part company with Lot. Lot had come a long way with Abraham. But the vision of the city wasn't in his heart. He had glimpsed no glory and dreamed no dream. Stirred by the sense of adventure, feeling that anything was better than the boredom of life in Ur, he had gone along with the prophet of God. But he is willing to settle for short-term gains, unwilling to pay the price of the long-term objective. "Charismatic" means for him a pepped-up denominational worship service, house groups grafted onto the same old structure, a few choruses borrowed from the pioneers squeezed into the morning meeting. Enjoying the spin-offs of what God is doing but not committed to its vision; this is the Lot-mentality.

Abraham eventually had to bear the pain of parting from Lot. "He lived in tents, as did Isaac and Jacob, who were heirs with him of the same promise" (Heb. 11:9). Not all fellow-travellers are fellow-heirs. We learn this to our cost as we try to live up to the light we have received.

(iii) *Vision will make me dissatisfied with anything man has built*
Abraham was "looking forward to the city with foundations, whose architect and builder is God" (Heb. 11:10). Nothing that is temporal, traditional or sectarian will do for leaders with God-given vision. They are willing to be non-conformist for the sake of it. They may make trouble for themselves because they will try to administer in the Church only those principles that are compatible with the final heading up of all things in Christ (cf. Eph. 1:10). They will be able to tear themselves away from churches or work to which they have given long years of envisioning. They will do this for the sake of the vision that is bigger than anything that has been accomplished. Without owning an inch of the land, Abraham rejoices in all of it as his inheritance (Acts 7:5)! "Lift up your eyes from where you are … (Gen. 13:14). And what do we see for ourselves?" said Campbell Morgan. "Nothing of the success we may have desired in our leadership. Yet everything of the land, the fulfilment of all our dreams and the ultimate glory is ours even as we look again. It is glorious to do without and still to have by sharing in the process that moves towards God's final victory."[3]

Revelation and vision are then vital to leadership and their price is well worth paying. As leaders we consistently need the Spirit of wisdom and revelation which Paul sought for the Ephesians. The Spirit will reveal to us further dimensions and directions in the hope of our calling. "I pray that your inner vision may be flooded with light, to enable you to see what hope the fact that he has called you gives you" (Eph. 1:18, William Barclay).

Notes

1. D.M. Lloyd-Jones, *Romans: an exposition of Chapter 8:5–17 "The Sons of God"* (Edinburgh: The Banner of Truth Trust, 1974), especially chapters 25–27.
2. Oswald Chambers, *So Send I You* (London: Marshall, Morgan, and Scott, 1930/1964), p.33.
3. Campbell Morgan, *Westminster Sermons* Vol 10 (London: Pickering and Inglis), p.248.

CHAPTER EIGHT

No Plastic Prophets

Once upon a time someone, somewhere, poured a huge bucket of cold water over the emotional life of leaders. Cool, calm and collected is the rigid image of a leader in many people's minds. Within living memory, a presidential candidate in the United States put himself out of the running by weeping in public. The Church has not been immune from this. For a long time we took our leaders straight out of the deep freeze and wondered why our Christianity was so cold and uninspiring. The Holy Spirit is now showing us that it need not be, nor has it always been, like this with God's leaders.

The story is told of an American tourist in the nineteenth century visiting Robert Murray M'Cheyne's church in Dundee. Standing in the pulpit at St Peter's he asked an old janitor who remembered M'Cheyne to show him how the godly man preached. Advice was given. Holding the Bible in the way M'Cheyne had done, adopting his posture and stance, the tourist asked the janitor if there was anything else he needed to do. "Yes, there is," replied the old man, "now weep!" Without the tears the picture would have been incomplete.

The call of Moses to be the deliverer of Israel has already taken our attention. But it is important to see that behind the emergence of Moses lie the emotions of God Himself. " 'I have indeed seen the misery of my people in Egypt. I have heard them crying out because of their slave drivers, and I am concerned about their suffering' " (Exod. 3:7 cf. 2:23–25). God is not unmoved by His people's plight; He is feeling their hurt and sharing their pain. Because God is emotionally affected by the distress of His people He raises up a man to lead them out who will not only do what He says but who will feel what He feels. Centuries after Moses, Ezra shared the feelings of God over Israel's idolatry. "When I heard this, I tore my tunic and cloak, pulled hair from my head and beard and sat down appalled" (Ezra 9:3). Clearly here is one leader not at this point cool, calm and collected! Nehemiah's reaction is similar. Hearing of the distress of the remnant struggling to re-establish itself in the land, Nehemiah felt his heart breaking within him! "When I heard these things, I sat down and wept. For some days I mourned ..." (Neh. 1:4). The man of God is not only filled with human sympathy for the people but is sharing the reproach and shame God feels at the disgrace of His people. For an Israel that has, for the moment, rejected her Messiah but is still the object of covenant-love, Paul feels in his heart "great sorrow and unceasing anguish" (Rom. 9:2). In every respect this is a far cry from stiff upper lip leadership!

Prophetic emotions

Of all God's gifts of ministry, it is *prophetic* leadership especially which is called to reflect God's feelings. Prophets are often called to grasp the twin terminals of man's sin and God's holiness and the shock to their system is usually acute. This should not excuse needlessly eccentric behaviour on the prophet's part but it does help to explain that certain mystery and strangeness which sometimes colours this ministry. *For the prophet is not just a bearer but an embodiment of the Word God gives*. The prophet is called therefore to convey not only the message but the feelings of God to His people. The great Jewish scholar, Abraham Heschel, roots the subjective side of the prophetic calling in what he calls "*pathos*".[1] The prophet, he says, enters into an emotional communion with God's feelings as well as God's Word, for both are part of God's truth. This is illustrated by the ministry of Elisha. Foreseeing what the ruthless Hazael will do to Israel when he succeeds Ben-Hadad as king of Syria, Elisha predicts the king's immediate recovery and subsequent death. The prophet fully realises the implications of his words. Burdened with this terrible knowledge he breaks down in front of Hazael. "He stared at him with a fixed gaze until Hazael felt ashamed. Then the man of God began to weep" (2 Kings 8:11). This is not sentimentality but sympathy with God and is itself an expression of how God puts His heart into His Word. This is the Word burning like fire in Jeremiah; the Word that breaks his heart and intoxicates his whole being (Jer. 23:9,29). *Without the Word pathos is just pathetic; but with the Word pathos is prophetic.*

Uniquely among the prophets it is Hosea who most embodies this. His own intensely personal domestic anguish becomes itself the moving parable of God's heartache over adulterous Israel. For Hosea it was not what he thought but what he suffered that made him a prophet. We are not called today to such terrible enactments of the Word for the incarnation has upstaged all prophetic symbolism. But we are called as leaders to lay down our lives for God's Word, even if only in instalments. It is our calling to feel what God feels and to communicate something of this to the people of God. We are to do this even when it entails withstanding the emotions of the people, as Paul and Agabus did, that God's Word might be fulfilled (Acts 21). Feeling what God feels, at least in measure, will affect how we speak for Him. Our prophecies do not come through playback machines but through people. No one loathes more than I do the phony religious confidence or quavering voice that tries to bolster prophetic utterance. But our words for God should carry conviction and convey feelings. When God speaks He is not reading from the telephone directory!

In Richard Baxter's words, "If you give the holy things of God the highest praises in words and yet do it coldly, you will seem in the manner to unsay what you said in the matter. The manner as well as the words must set them forth ... that the people can *feel* us preach when they hear us."[2] Because prophets embody the Word as well as bear it, their sensitivities are opened to a wider range of experience than others. Prophetic people may be more prone to fluctuations of feeling and mood than others, more liable to hear discordant notes, because their ears are tuned to grander harmonies. Enlarge this vision and they become more prone to impatience and disillusionment. Elijah is a case in point. In the inevitable psychological anti-climax that followed the spiritual "Everest" of his encounter with the false prophets of Baal, the prophet is especially vulnerable. Nervously exhausted, Elijah is open to the spiritual attack and emotional manipulation of Jezebel. He lapses into self-pity and abject despair, feelings so at odds with his very recent faith and boldness on Mount Carmel.

The Lord's first answer to this state of mind in His prophet is typically wise and gracious. The Lord gives Elijah just what he needs, which is not a refresher course in theology or an intense counselling session but a square meal and a sound sleep! Then to the slowly recovering but still fragile heart of His prophet the Lord speaks, not with earthquake, wind or fire – any of which might have blown Elijah's emotional fuses yet again – but with a quiet word in his ear. The dramatic natural phenomena may have reactivated Elijah's jaded awareness but at this point the Lord knew how to get through to His man in a winning way.

The prophetic temperament is to be taken into account here. Prophets are tested for their character but not judged for their temperament. It is just this variety of temperament in God's messengers that helps Him colour in His Word and shows us that His wisdom is a many-splendoured thing. Could a more self-confident man than Jeremiah have borne such universal rejection? When you think the worst of yourself what can man say of you that can hurt your feelings? Self-deprecation may have proved the deepest, if strangest, safeguard for a prophet called to a ministry of almost total unpopularity. Today, however, Jeremiah would more likely have been deemed a suitable case for treatment, been disqualified from ministry and made a candidate for inner healing. To attain emotional wholeness is a fine aim but we do well to set it just below a sight of God in all His glory as our chief ambition. For this Isaiah lost his well-integrated life – becoming ruined as he put it – but in doing so he gained his prophetic soul.

Stirring the people

All this is especially significant when we see that it is the role of prophetic leadership to stir up the people of God. Unresponsiveness in God's people is still the greatest barrier to the supernatural and miraculous breaking forth among us. Responsiveness is not merely, or chiefly, a matter of psychology, of course; the spirit and mind and will are essential in this. But emotional sluggishness is a bigger hindrance to spiritual advance than we often recognise. We lack emotional awareness and stamina, scarcely able to sustain a lengthy period of praise without sitting down and bowing out. The early Billy Graham crusades were often criticised for being too emotional. With hindsight we might well come to exactly the opposite conclusion – that they were not emotional enough. If there were drop-outs from the conversion line, it was surely due to lack of emotional commitment not excess of it. Too many perhaps, when decision time came, at an artificially contrived moment, voted with their feet but not their hearts.

This emotional sluggishness is reinforced by the over-bombardment of our senses in an electronic age. Media exposure to tragedy, for example, has undoubtedly numbed our senses and dulled our reactions. Pictures of starving children no longer move us because we don't know what to do with the useless feelings they raise. The sight of so much tragedy far-removed from the sounds and smells of real events has devalued pain. In much the same way an over-diet of shoddy entertainment has trivialised pleasure. We are over-exposed to relentlessly unfunny comedy shows and the synthetic heartiness of media personalities which, like the advertising that sponsors them, promise more than they deliver. Canned laughter is an apt symbol of our age. Why not canned crying? Emotionally anaesthetised, we know neither true joy nor true sorrow. All of this finds subtle reinforcement in our natural English horror of enthusiasm. Being English we prefer understatement to bold speech, oblique hints to direct talk. We rightly suspect exaggeration, ballyhoo and presumption. We recoil instinctively from brashness and hype. But behind the sometimes extravagant extraversion that characterises the personality types of some flamboyant leaders may lie a passion to generate a response from people, to rouse them from their spectator-sport to faith, action and involvement. This is not confusing grace and works; merely distinguishing between being passive and being receptive.

If we want to do better than this and avoid spurious or even dubious practices then we will need true prophetic leaders genuinely moved with holy wrath or pure compassion and able to stir the people to a true response. Then the sound of true sorrow and true joy may well be mixed (Ezra 3:12–13). Then the freshly moved leader will communicate new stirrings to the people. "So the Lord stirred up the spirit of Zerubbabel ... and the spirit of the whole remnant of the people. They came and began work on the house of the Lord Almighty, their God" (Hag. 1:14). This is not just keeping up morale by some technique of positive confession or positive thinking but a genuine warming of the hearts of the people by a fresh encounter with the living God, who through His prophet confirms that He is with them. Through the prophet we learn that the tragedy *of* the world is more grievous than the tragedy *in* the world. Through the prophetic voice we learn that the pleasures for evermore at God's right hand are there to be increasingly and unendingly appreciated by all who in redemption have rediscovered their reason for living in worshipping God and enjoying Him for ever.

What is clear is that prophets themselves need emotional refreshment in order to lead God's people in this way. They have to be stirred again and again. Easily bored with what is less than God's best, they must stir themselves constantly if they are not to become critics or, worse, cynics. To do this and to find fresh inspiration Elisha called for music and a minstrel (2 Kings 3:15), while David remonstrated with himself and roused his own soul (Psa. 42). The company of colleagues is a great stimulus here. Paul is glad to acknowledge that others had "refreshed his spirit" (1 Cor. 16:18; cf. 2 Cor. 7:6,13) and that Onesiphorus had been like a cool breeze to him by the freshness of his fellowship.

To know this joy, leaders need unrestrained affections. Paul's affection for the elders at Ephesus and theirs for him make for one of the most moving passages in the New Testament (Acts 20). "With humility and tears" Paul had served the Lord among them; "with tears" he had spent three years in close pastoral admonition and love. No wonder these men loved him in return and were not ashamed to show it. Not a stiff upper lip anywhere. Kneeling together in fervent prayer on the quayside, arms round each other, kisses everywhere, tears streaming down softened faces – these are New Testament leaders and this was a "leaders' meeting"! And not a notebook or clip board in sight. Let brotherly, and sisterly, love continue.

Notes

1. Abraham Heschel, *The Prophets* (New York: Harper and Row, 1975), p.88.
2. Richard Baxter, *The Reformed Pastor* (London: Epworth Press, 1656/1961), p.106.

CHAPTER NINE

Man after God's Heart

More than anyone else in the Old Testament, the man who sets the standard for leadership is David. Subsequent kings were measured by him. For "walking in the ways of David" Josiah was commended; for failing to do so Ahaz was condemned. Many centuries later, Israel's leaders in restoration, Ezra and Nehemiah, were still carefully following what had been "prescribed by David, king of Israel" (Ezra 3:10; Neh. 12:24). It is David who is prophetically set forth as the model for Messiahship (Ezek. 34:20–24) fulfilled in his "greater", in fact greatest, son. David's leadership was so symbolically and strategically important that it is surprising how little attention he is given in manuals of biblical leadership.

His leadership is wide-ranging in its lessons and far-reaching in its implications. David deserves the study of every leader of the people of God.

Generation game

Before all this greatness intimidates us we can take heart from Paul's assessment of David's rule. Speaking to the synagogue congregation in Antioch Paul tells us that "David had served God's purpose in his own generation" (Acts 13:36). This is all the more heartening to us for being so prosaic. However strategic David's leadership was to prove in God's plans in history, it is merely said of him here that he did what he could for God in the time that he had. Although David's leadership, prophetically, had implications for the future which we in our day are enjoying, it is heartening to realise that he was content also to be a man of his time, serving eternal plans going far beyond the limits of his lifetime. Much of what he envisaged as God's work for him he did not in fact achieve. Another built his temple for him. A lesser man than David might have become frustrated or cynical so that his later energies drained away in disillusionment. David did not let this happen. Much of what was promised him, as he realised, was for a "distant future" (2 Sam. 7:19). Being a man of faith, however, he did not become an idle dreamer, considering the affairs of the present to be beneath him, too mundane to be bothered with. Leaders, especially those with great vision, need to watch that they do not become so high-minded as to be of no earthly use.

Paul adds of David that "he fell asleep" *after* having served God in his generation; not, we might add, *during* it as some leaders of the people do! As a leader David was wide awake to every opportunity to serve the living God. His repeated "I will awake the dawn" is typical of a man who can't wait to maximise the moments of today with tomorrow in view. This is second nature to any farmer for whom there is no reaping tomorrow without sowing today and who is wise enough not to allow long-term aims to paralyse present activity.

The secret of this alertness as of every other aspect of David's leadership is that he was "a man after God's own heart". Looking on the heart not on the outward appearances which impress us so much, God picks the man to lead whose heart is set on doing His will (1 Sam. 13:14; 16:7; Acts 13:22). Two features especially of this "heart set on God" are relevant for leaders.

(i) David is presented to us as having a *wholeness of heart*, a single-minded commitment to the will of God as he understands it. This whole-heartedness was meant to be emulated by his son, Solomon, but sadly wasn't. "As Solomon grew old ... his heart was not fully devoted to the Lord his God, as the heart of David his father had been" (1 Kings 11:4; cf. 1 Kings 9:4). Undoubtedly though it was this very quality in David which others with leadership strength found compelling. Double-mindedness wins few worthwhile followers. David, on the other hand, was able to ask others to make sacrifices for God because he would never himself offer to God anything which cost him nothing. "No, I insist on paying the full price," he presses Aruanah when the latter offers to give him the threshing-floor for nothing as a site for the altar. Later, when costly giving is required of the people, David as their leader has the moral authority to ask for it. "Who is willing to consecrate himself today to the Lord?" First to step forward were David's fellow-leaders who gave lavishly towards the work of the temple. "The people rejoiced at the willing response of their leaders, for they had given freely and wholeheartedly to the Lord" (1 Chron. 21:24, 29:5–9).

(ii) David is pictured as demonstrating an *integrity of heart* we do well as leaders to prize. Asaph who was close enough to David to know otherwise testified to this feature of David's rule over Israel and praised God for it. "And David shepherded them with integrity of heart; with skilful hands he led them" (Psa. 78:72). The skill was in safe hands because the heart was sound. Sinless, David certainly wasn't but he could claim to know the blessedness of being a guileless man (Psa. 32). As a leader with his fair share of sin and mistakes he nevertheless kept short accounts with God and was honoured for it. A clear conscience, as Paul so frequently reminds us, frees us from crippling self-analysis, to do the work of God with clear intent, leaving judgement on ourselves to the Lord. This is a leader's best vindication. "Our sole defence is a life of integrity" (2 Cor. 6:7, Phillips).

In all this David was, as Stephen later described him, "greatly favoured by the Lord". Being a forgiven man David knew what it was to live under grace. The freedom he was given in leadership was unusual, a certain sign of God's favour. Almost uniquely, David at various times was enabled to be prophet, priest and king. Where others had been condemned for usurping the restricted role of the priest, David was granted diplomatic immunity as a herald of the coming kingdom of Jesus (cf. Mark 2:24–26). It was said of him that "the Lord helped him wherever he went" so much was the grace of God on his leadership. Leaders with the favour and grace of God resting on them can expect to be extended and enlarged in their sphere of ministry. Surprising skills and surprising scope are given to any leader who is moving in the fullness of God's blessing.

Last words

For further light on the matter in hand we turn to David's swansong recorded for us in the twenty-third chapter of the second book of Samuel. David's last words are not the last word on leadership but they are magnificently practical. From them we make a number of points.

(i) He is proud to be known as *"the son of Jesse"* (2 Sam. 23:1). The family had been David's first school of leadership. The youngest of nine brothers, David learned not to let any false inhibition hinder him or big brother deter him. When David turns up to deal with the giant Goliath he is roughly handled by his eldest brother Eliab. "What are you doing around here, anyway? ... What about the sheep you're supposed to be taking care of? I know what a cocky brat you are; you just want to watch the battle!" (1 Sam. 17:28, TLB). Undaunted, David keeps asking how long they are prepared to let this pagan giant taunt the armies of the living God. Any leader who feels their family background counts against them in any way can take heart from this. No childhood oppression or adolescent disadvantage can ultimately thwart God's call in a leader's life.

In the family, too, David had learned the principle which Jesus later laid down so clearly as a rule for leaders in His kingdom. We shall have occasion to notice this again. Suffice it to say here that David learned his leadership by first being faithful in small and natural things. Faithful in caring for a flock of sheep, he is made shepherd of a nation. Faithful in tending what belonged to someone else, he is given responsibility for his own. Faithful in protecting the flock against lions and bears, he is given grace to protect the people of God against Goliath and deliver them from hostile nations.

(ii) He never forgets that he has been *raised to eminence by God* (2 Sam. 23:1). Never forgetting his roots, knowing where he's come from, he never ceases to marvel at having come so far and having attained so high a place. Never ceasing to wonder at this, he gives God all the credit. He knows himself to be a man "exalted by God" who owes his rise to fame and leadership only to the Lord. David is no self-appointed leader. Not originally the people's choice but God's, he is never in danger of self-congratulation. "Who am I and what is my house that you should treat me as a man of high standing?" is his attitude when talking to God (1 Chron. 17:17). And when talking to the people he reminds them that it was God's pleasure not theirs which had made him king (1 Chron. 28:4). He could sing from experience that God exalts the humble but abases the proud, that such decisions are in divine hands and that it is God's condescension which makes a man great (Psa. 75:6; 18:35). David was a leader who never got above himself – except that is when he was in trouble; then he knew there was always one rock higher to climb to (Psa. 61:2)! Likewise any leader who is confident in being God's choice can have the same blend of boldness and humility, able to rise above even the "contentions of the people" (2 Sam. 22:44). Such leaders know their place in God's order because they have heeded the counsel: "Do not think of yourself more highly than you ought, but rather think of yourself with sober judgment" (Rom. 12:3). Neither over- nor underestimating themselves they can fulfil their calling to lead with a sense of security and purpose.

(iii) He knows himself to be the man *"anointed* by the God of Jacob" (2 Sam. 23:1). David looks back across the years to his original anointing to be Israel's leader. "So Samuel took the horn of oil and anointed him in the presence of his brothers, and from that day on the Spirit of the Lord came upon David in power" (1 Sam. 16:13). Even before he had come to his own kingship he had felt by the Spirit an instinctive respect for the spiritual authority of the Lord's anointed, Saul. Saul's bad example did nothing to dull this sense in David of the vital importance of God's anointing on a leader's life. It was the one thing above all else that marked him out as having the right to rule. In this anointing David rejoiced continually. "He shows unfailing kindness to his anointed" (Psa. 18:50). "You anoint my head with oil; my cup overflows" (Psa. 23:5). He looks to this to iron out the inconsistencies in his life. "May your good Spirit lead me on level ground" (Psa. 143:10).

Always dependent on the anointing of the Holy Spirit David rejoices when it is freshly given: "fine oils have been poured upon me" (Psa. 92:10). Certainly in these days of spiritual renewal, we recognise our absolute reliance on the Holy Spirit to make our leadership valid. Apart from asking for forgiveness, there is no prayer I pray more often as a leader than David's own heart-cry: "Do not take your Holy Spirit from me" (Psa. 51:11). Only the Holy Spirit can qualify us for leadership. Only He can make good the defects that sin exposes in us – the need for a cleaner heart, a more steadfast and willing spirit (Psa. 51:10–12). In short, as we have seen in an earlier chapter, the Holy Spirit's anointing is essential for leadership. Astonished often by what we accomplish with this anointing of the Spirit, alarmed to the point of terror at the thought of losing it, we share David's feelings.

(iv) He is a *worshipper*, "Israel's singer of songs" (2 Sam. 23:1). David is the singer of songs for all seasons, songs of pain and pleasure wrung out of him by the intensity and intimacy of his life with God. David is the psalmist who tugs at the heart-strings of every mood in the spiritual life. Singing, shouting, silent, wondering, clapping, dancing, David ransacks the whole repertoire of response to bless his God. To be a leader is to be first and foremost a worshipper. David shows us what Ezekiel later explained more fully, that the first privilege and first priority of God's leaders is their "ministry unto the Lord" (Ezek. 44). Ministering to the Lord precedes ministry to His people. Every leader needs to know that ministering to the house of God in work for His people is no substitute for ministering to the heart of God in worship of Him alone. The first leaders of the Early Church knew the secret, for it was "While they were worshipping the Lord and fasting, the Holy Spirit said, 'Set apart for me Barnabas and Saul' " (Acts 13:2).

We read in 1 Chronicles 15 of the care and creativity with which David set out his directions for worship. Leaving the Mosaic tabernacle with its prescribed animal sacrifices at Gibeon, he built a tabernacle in Jerusalem solely for continuous praise and worship. It was an incredible trailer for the spiritual worship of the coming kingdom of Jesus. The praise the Holy Spirit is now drawing from so many today is no passing fad. It is modelled on the very worship David was prophetically given to offer as a foretaste of praise in the kingdom. His leadership here was therefore of immense prophetic significance. Nothing will make us more surely people "after God's own heart" in our own day than becoming leaders like David of the prophetic praise of the people of God.

(v) He recalls with relish that *the Spirit of the Lord spoke through me* (2 Sam. 23:2). Every leader called in some measure to be God's mouthpiece will savour the experience which David here describes. In his relationship to revelation, of course, David, as part of God's infallible Word, stands apart from us. Knowing what forgiveness is at first hand, he can be the prophet of justification by faith (Psa. 32; Rom.

4:6–8). Looking ahead down the centuries, as Peter later pictured him, David becomes the prophet of a rescue from death and ascension to glory which only the resurrection and exaltation of his greater son can fulfil (Acts 2:25–35). While none of us can claim the Spirit's inspiration in such a way or for such a range, we all need to know, whether for public preaching or private counselling, that His word is on our tongues (2 Sam. 23:2). The leader who listens to God before talking to the people is more likely to gain an audience. In this way we may aspire to David's retrospective confidence that "the Spirit of the Lord spoke through me". Today's leadership, as never before, knows that worn-out clichés heal no wounds. Apart from the gift of prophecy there have been no gifts I have more earnestly desired of the Holy Spirit than His words of wisdom and knowledge. Just occasionally I think I've been sensible enough not to lean on my own understanding entirely but to let Him get His word in edgeways. To make David's claim my own all I need, in common with other leaders, is that what is occasional should become habitual. Then I too might be able to say as a servant of God, that "The Sovereign Lord has given me an instructed tongue, to know the word that sustains the weary. He wakens me morning by morning, wakens my ear to listen like one being taught" (Isa. 50:4). Only a warm bed, it seems, stands between me and being a prophet!

The Lord has the last word

Not least among the benefits of hearing God speak is that of learning His views on leadership! In David's last words, the last word on leadership is spoken by God. For all the benefit we derive from secular sources on management techniques, leadership training, the art of delegation and counselling and so on, this is not where we begin or end. The writing of this book has behind it the clear desire to let God define leadership for us.

A true leader is one who "*rules… in righteousness … in the fear of God*" (2 Sam. 23:3).

No one can be a leader among God's people whose leadership is not rooted in an encounter with the Holy One of Israel. "The Lord confides in those who fear him" (Psa. 25:14). At the heart of Messiah's spiritual authority and of all who are His delegates is the "Spirit of knowledge and of the fear of the Lord" (Isa. 11:2). This fear will be a delight not a dread and it sets us free from superficial or partial judgements. Decisions are then made not on the basis of the way things seem but on the way things are (Isa. 11:3–5). "He shall draw breath in the fear of God" (George Adam Smith). Throughout his reign David exemplifies this, making few moves, except the wrong ones, without entering the presence of the Lord for permission. "David enquired of the Lord" (2 Sam. 2:1). "David sought the face of the Lord" (2 Sam. 21:1). Because he was sensitive to God's wisdom David discovered the different stratagem needed on each occasion to bring him victory (2 Sam. 5).

Ruling in the fear of God enabled David to accept God's "no" to his own plans and prevented resentment or negativism from taking root in his life. When things do not work out exactly in the way we had hoped or planned, we who live in the fear of God will not react like spoiled children. Forbidden by the prophetic word to build the temple he had set his heart on, David comes before the Lord in moving simplicity. "He sat before the Lord" – a delightful image showing us that the fear of God is not a craven or cringing attitude but the relaxed and restful humility of a son before his Father. "Who am I, O Sovereign Lord, and what is my family, that you have brought me this far? And as if this were not enough in your sight, O Sovereign Lord, you have also spoken about the future of the house of your servant" (2 Sam. 7:18–19). God's plans, as David found, are always bigger than ours; what is in His heart is always much grander than what is in ours. Knowing this, leaders who cherish the fear of God will not be peeved to learn the true scale of their own contribution to God's cause but only proud to feel that they have a part to play at all in the grand scheme of things. The fear of the Lord gives both a healthy sense of proportion and a hopeful sense of significance to our best efforts.

Ruling in the fear of God also enables David to take responsibility for his sins and mistakes, for the lust that claims Bathsheba and the pride that numbers the people. Fearing God, David shows a readiness to confess and repent. "I am the man, Nathan; you are right, I have sinned." Fearing God with a trembling trust, David submits to God's wrath over the census of Israel, never doubting for a moment that he would sooner take judgement from God than take his chance with men (2 Sam. 24:10–25). In leadership, for sure, the fear of the Lord is the beginning of wisdom. It is this fear that makes us play to God as our audience and frees us from the self-consciousness encouraged by the criticism of others, especially of those closest to us.

When David returned home to bless his household, Michal daughter of Saul came out to meet him and said, "How the king of Israel has distinguished himself today, disrobing in the sight of the slave girls of his servants as any vulgar fellow would."

David said to Michal, "It was before the Lord, who chose me rather than your father or anyone from his house when he appointed me ruler over the Lord's people Israel – I will celebrate before the Lord."

(2 Sam. 6:20–21)

God's blessing on the leadership which fears Him is poetically described. "When he rules in the fear of God, he is like the light of morning at sunrise on a cloudless morning, like the brightness after rain that brings the grass from the earth" (2 Sam. 23:3–4).

With this lovely description of its effect surely no one can doubt that leadership is a good thing!

I see from it that God-fearing leadership *brings fresh hope* to people. With the dawn of a new day people's hopes of a new start rise. Such a leader will bring a keenness to the air around him. Others will find such leadership and presence invigorating. Coming to a situation that has been locked up in despair or weary resignation an anointed leader can bring a fresh sense of well-being, making people feel again, in a way impossible to articulate, that it is good to be alive. Onesiphorus in this way was able to refresh Paul. "Many times did that man put fresh heart into me," says the apostle. "His visits revived me like a breath of fresh air" (2 Tim. 1:16, Phillips/TLB). God-fearing leadership *brings cleanness to the atmosphere around*. Unresolved issues that have become stale and mouldy are dealt with. Situations on which the door of fear has been shut so that they have become musty have fresh air let into them. The moral atmosphere seems suddenly cleaner and healthier and the spiritual air sweeter and sounder. A leader ruling in the fear of the Lord will be a moral antiseptic to any community and one which lasts (cf. Psa. 19:9).

God-fearing leadership *brings a new clarity to life* like a rainwashed sky in the morning sun. It sharpens the thinking of God's people. Others begin to see things in a new light because the leader seeks to live in the light of God.

God-fearing leadership *brings a new impartation of energy*. As grass starts to grow in the sunshine that follows rain so things start to happen when a person who rules in the fear of the Lord takes charge. Things start moving again. People start to grow and develop and become fruitful under such leadership. When people become weary in well-doing, such a leader can arouse them to new achievements, as Haggai did to the dispirited remnant rebuilding Jerusalem.

All these things David to some measure exemplifies. As a result his house is ordered and secure and prospering (2 Sam. 23:5). There is no place in it for the unsubmissive, for those who refuse to be taken in hand (23:6). Any leader willing to be taken in hand by the fear of God will however bring the dawning of a new day to the Church's life.

David is a model for leadership not least because at the end of his rule he can still sing about it! And God has pledged His prophetic word to have more "shepherds after my own heart" (Jer. 3:15). Being awed by God but not over-awed by David, we can take heart as leaders from Zechariah's promise that "the feeblest among them will be like David" (Zech. 12:8)!

CHAPTER TEN

Two are Better than One

Leadership should properly be listed as a collective noun. The apostles, let's not forget, went into the world as the animals went into the ark – two by two! As leaders we are not called to "go solo" all the time. "Plurality" is the rather ugly word that has recently attached itself to this principle, but a rose by any other name is just as sweet and the concept of shared leadership is nowadays becoming more widely appreciated and applied. "For waging war you need guidance, and for victory many advisers" (Prov. 24:6). The news that the ministry is no longer a "one-man band" has come as a glorious relief to many, not least to those in the so-called "full-time" ministry. My fellow leaders have been a great joy to me as I have sought to fulfil my ministry.

When I have needed genuine appreciation it has best come from other leaders on a peer-level whose recognition really counts because it is honest and objective. When I have needed support it has been there. When I have needed correction or adjustment it has usually come from the Lord through them. Proverbs deftly describes the way that admonition can get past our defences when given by a friend we trust – "wounds from a friend can be trusted" (Prov. 27:6). The mental and spiritual stimulus of meeting with other leaders is one of the chief delights of shared ministry. "As iron sharpens iron, so one man sharpens another" (Prov. 27:17). I have never found my own role inhibited by this but rather enlarged and enhanced. In fact I suspect that only in such a plurality do we begin to find out who and what we are in God. No one loses authority by shared leadership. Rather my own measure of God-given authority was reinforced in the eyes of the people when they realised and later saw that behind me were other servants of God whose backing they could trust. No longer did they feel that I was a maverick, riding my own particular hobbyhorse of vision and strategy but a true representative among many others of what God was saying to His Church. This threatened some of course and called their bluff. But for most it was a welcome reassurance and only served to increase my respect among the people.

These obvious gains from shared ministry and the fact that leaders lose nothing by opening their life and ministry to each other, should not minimise the cost. "Its obvious price," as Derek Kidner so aptly puts it, "is a person's independence; henceforth he must consult another's interest and convenience, listen to another's reasoning, adjust to another's pace and style, keep faith with another's trust."[1] As I began tentatively to put this maxim into practice, meetings with other leaders both within and beyond the local church took top priority in my diary. These times together were not regarded as luxuries in my timetable, a welcome but non-essential break from the real work of ministry. On the contrary, I came to see them as strategic and essential to the work of God in our day. For the same reason, the personal enjoyment and strength gained from such relationships should not be taken to imply that they are optional, intended only for the weak in faith or poor in gift. What we are describing in fact is a provision and pattern for leadership which has strong biblical support.

The need for leadership to be shared is perhaps most vividly seen in the ministry of Moses. This can be viewed *from the outside*, as it were, looking in – and then, from the inside as we feel the pressure Moses is under. Exodus 18 views the need in Moses' life from the outside through the eyes of Jethro, his father-in-law. Jethro is heard remonstrating with Moses. "What do you think you are? A one man band? Look at yourself, you're exhausted and I'm not a bit surprised! Have you seen how long those queues are outside the counselling tent? All day some of them have been there; they weren't too pleased when we put the 'closed' sign up tonight. Some of them are still out there waiting for us to open up in the morning. But, Moses, there are a lot of frustrated people out there. I'm telling you, it's not good, Moses. What are you up to? Is this a DIY-counselling service or something? Listen to me, Moses! Why are you trying to do it on your own? It's not good for them and it's not good for you. You'll wear yourself out and you'll wear them out! Don't you see, you can't handle this on your own? Take a piece of advice from your old father-in-law, son ..." And thankfully, Moses did take Jethro's advice.

What Jethro said was a word in season, in a situation near to getting out of hand. He told Moses three things.

(i) Talk more to God about the people than to the people about their problems (Exod. 18:21). Your wisdom would be worth more if you did and some problems would disappear immediately.

(ii) Teach the people more clearly to walk in God's ways. Many of them will stop being parasitic on your wisdom and good nature and will begin to stand on their own two feet, mature enough to discern for themselves between good and evil (Exod. 18:20; cf. Heb. 5:14).

and, above all –
(iii) Delegate responsibility to others and share the burden of pastoral leadership with them (Exod. 18:21).

The word of the Lord through Jethro even spelt out the kind of helpers Moses was to select to stand with him in leadership. They were to have ability, and be capable of ruling over and caring for the people. They were to be God-fearing, with a godliness which matched their gifts; they were to be passionate for truth, keen to bring matters into the light of God's Word; people who would neither be bribed nor corrupted; humble people willing to serve at different levels of responsibility without envy or competitiveness.

In turn these co-workers were not to be left without the oversight of Moses but in disputes which demanded too much of them could have recourse to "higher authority" by bringing the issue to him. Such "plurality" works! Moses can now endure pressure, his nervous breakdown avoided; the people can now enjoy peace, their rebellious breakout averted! All in all a recipe for righteousness and rest for leader and people.

The priesthood of other believers

For a view of a similar situation *from the inside* we turn to Numbers chapter 11. Here we see that behind the cheerful bedside manner lurks a smouldering irritation not to say resentment. The door bell rings as the family sits down to dinner. "Hope it's not an inconvenient time to call?" "Not at all, come right in; how can I help?" As far as Moses is concerned it's one time too many! Later with the gritted teeth relaxed, he lets God have it. "Why pick on me, Lord? What did I do to get landed with this lot? Whose children are they anyway? Am I their father? Surely I don't have to spoon-feed them all the time? Do I have to carry them personally into Canaan? Sorry, Lord, it's just not on; I can't cope with it all. It's killing me; I'll be dead and buried before I'm a hundred at this rate. It's not fair; it's an impossible situation."

Let's face it we've all been there haven't we? What's more to the point is that the pressure on Moses reflects a pressure on the people. Over this the "anger of the Lord was kindled" (Num. 11:10). Sensing this divine concern, Moses reacts defensively and lets his self-pity boil over.

Once again God's answer is *delegated responsibility*. Seventy men are given a measure of the Spirit which rests on Moses for rule and leadership. Because Moses is also a prophet they receive the Spirit of prophecy as a bonus (Num. 11:25). Moses now has Spirit-filled assistants who can share the weight of leadership with him. Any doubts Moses had felt at his inability to meet the needs of so large a company of people are subdued by this dynamic move of God to meet his own need for help. Because his own load has been lightened, and being a prophet, Moses is given to see in prophetic yearning a yet future company of God's people in whom the prophethood and priesthood is opened to all believers. What it is to lead among such a people Moses was not to know but we do. As leaders in the Body of Christ and as leaders together of a microcosm of it, we know the relief of being able to "bear one another's burdens" for this is the law and the Spirit of Christ to us (Gal. 6:1f.). Without this one is left to conclude that "all labour and achievement spring from man's envy of his neighbour" (Eccl. 4:4). This competitive spirit can be overcome only in a community where each is willing to serve the other for a common end. The loner is in danger not only of being competitive but also of being compulsive. This is the person who needs to question the point of such prodigious self-effort: "There was a man all alone; he had neither son nor brother. There was no end to his toil, yet his eyes were not content with his wealth. 'For whom am I toiling,' he asked, 'and why am I depriving myself of enjoyment?'" (Eccl. 4:8). For such people, work becomes an obsession precisely because there is no one dependent on them. Lacking relationships, they lose the point of what they are doing. But when an individual is willing to accept a share of corporate responsibilities that work immediately becomes meaningful. So shared leadership covers a multitude of sins. Above all it is more efficient. D.L. Moody once said, "I would rather set ten men to work than do the work of ten men!"

The effects of team leadership then are relished by every leader experiencing them. Solomon was right. "Two are better than one, because they have a good return for their work: if one falls down, his friend can help him up … Also, if two lie down together, they will keep warm. But how can one keep warm alone? Though one may be overpowered, two can defend themselves. A cord of three strands is not quickly broken" (Eccl. 4:9–12). Here in shared life is shared success, help, comfort, protection and strength.

(i) Here is "a good return for labour", an increased measure of success for those who share leadership. So Moses needs Aaron as his mouthpiece and Hur as the upholder of his praying arms, for Israel to prevail. Ezra is matched by Nehemiah and both need the prophets if the work is not to be left half-finished. Zechariah is the visionary ("I saw flying scrolls"); Haggai the practical prophet ("Go and chop wood"); each perfectly complements the other in a way that makes their joint success greater than the sum of what each could have achieved on his own.

(ii) Here is mutual support for "if one falls down his friend can lift him up". "At my first defence no one supported me but all deserted me," confesses Paul, regretting the lack of what he was normally used to. Elsewhere he greets Priscilla and Aquila as a leadership couple and fellow-workers who risked their necks for him (Rom. 16:3).

(iii) Here is the warmth of love and fellow-feeling for "How can one keep warm on his own?" Even for male leaders, the biblical precedent is clear and satisfying. "Jonathan became one in spirit with David, and he loved him as himself" (1 Sam. 18:1). In this deep bond of manly love, sealed in covenant, they find tremendous support and mutual delight. His life threatened by Saul, David constantly looks to his friend for help and rescue. When out in the cold it is to Jonathan he looks for warmth and welcome. "And Saul's son Jonathan went to David at Horesh and helped him to find strength in God" (1 Sam. 23:16). No wonder David mourned for Jonathan and for losing the comfort of a love which surpassed the love of women. Any leader who scorns this or is a stranger to it is the poorer for it. Paul for his part longs to see Timothy for without him his joy is halved (2 Tim. 1:4). Stephanas, Fortunatus and Achaicus have refreshed Paul's spirit (1 Cor. 16:18). And as for Titus what could be more moving and revealing of the true humanity the Holy Spirit creates among leaders than this: "I still had no peace of mind, because I did not find my brother Titus there", but later "God, who comforts the downcast, comforted us by the coming of Titus" (2 Cor. 2:13; 7:6).

(iv) Here is safety and defence for "two can defend themselves". This can be misused as a refuge of irresolution and a recipe for confusion. But, for all that, it remains true that "many advisors make victory sure" and plans succeed with many advisors (Prov. 11:14; 15:22). This is the wisdom from above which is "open to reason and willing to yield" (James 3:17). Here leaders can test their cherished plans and dreams on the sounding board of the team's discernment. After much debate and hard-thinking James announced that it "seemed good to us and to the Holy Spirit". So one or two prophets may judge the revelation purporting to be from God. In this way the leadership is saved from individual arrogance and error and the Body of Christ protected from the tyranny of the self-willed leader's private interpretation of what God is saying. For "no prophecy of Scripture came about by the prophet's own interpretation" (2 Pet.1:20). So the gathered prophets and teachers confirm the call of God in Paul and Barnabas (Acts. 13:1ff.), while the elders in concert confirm the gift for leadership becoming apparent in the young man Timothy (1 Tim. 4:14) by laying on of hands and prophetic utterance. In this submitting of our ideas and judgements to other leaders we find safeguards against deception and confidence for action. By submitting our intuitions to one another, we let in the fear of God which is the beginning of wisdom.

(v) Here finally is the secret of surprising strength for "a threefold cord cannot easily be broken". Sharing our leadership in the way we have described is not just a useful stratagem, a convenient tactic for making the church run more smoothly. In it there is a mysterious working of supernatural strength. "Where two or three come together in my name, there am I with them." And this is just the gathering of strength. For "if two of you on earth agree about anything you ask for, it will be done for you by my Father in heaven" (Matt. 18:19–20). Even in His unique agreement with the Father, Jesus admits to a reliance upon the same divine principle. "I am the one who testifies for myself; my other witness is the one who sent me – the Father" for "it is written that the testimony of two men is valid" (John 8:17). Jesus and the apostles had presumably walked past the lame man at the gate of the Temple many times until one day Peter and John felt within them and in the strength of their relationship, a mysterious agreement. "Look at us," they said, and out of the mouths of these two apostles, in a unity of faith, is established the truth that the Name of Jesus brings healing and salvation as no other name can do! Leaders in heart agreement form a partnership for power that we have scarcely begun to exploit.

Not another committee

So far so good. There is room only for a few cautions on the outworking of plurality amongst leaders. One is that we may rush into it too quickly, running the risk of being "hasty in the laying on of hands" (1 Tim. 5:22). Eager to grasp the principle, find the relief and enter into the power of shared leadership, we may act impetuously. To draw in too many co-leaders too soon simply in order to achieve a numerical "plurality" is self-defeating. Most of your time will be cut out solving problems among your hastily assembled leadership group. Too many leaders in this case spoil the broth. Their lack of gift may well make them unacceptable to the people; their lack of grace unworkable with as fellow leaders. Either way the desired effect is forestalled. The priesthood of all believers does not mean the leadership of just anyone, any more as we saw than it means the leadership of no one! Charismatic worship for example fails when there are too many ostensible "leaders" all "having a go", with the result that the people feel nagged rather than exhorted and become insecure, not knowing really who their shepherd is. Rush into a recognition of plurality and you risk denying the gifts and calling of God without which no man can be leader.

A second caution is one expressed by Charles Blair, failed leader of an early megachurch, who lost the safety in numbers which plurality should bring. "Are your co-workers a completion of yourself? Or simply an extension. If I am called to leadership and find helpers who are simply echoes of myself, I double my strengths but I also double my weaknesses."[2] Leaders who "measure themselves by themselves ... are not wise" (2 Cor. 10:12). Comparisons within our own circle are rarely odious and this is good but they need to be honest. As Rehoboam discovered, the views of some men you consult are not worth having because they merely echo your own immaturity (1 Kings 12:1ff.). Plurality needs to be a true meeting of ministries that are genuinely complementary to one another, not carbon copies of each other. This forges a relationship which is strong enough to allow a Paul to withstand a Peter to his face and not lose friendship.

Lastly, we must not let plurality blur the clarity that anointed leadership brings to a church. In an effort to be humble and submissive we may falsely try to play down our distinctive abilities and ministry. Like it or not, though all leaders are equal, some are more equal than others! It would be ironic to avoid the pitfalls of democratic church government only to fall into the trap of leadership by opinion-poll. We all know that a camel is a horse designed by a committee!

None of this should deter us from walking down the road of plural leadership for the gains are too good to miss. Concealed in this simple strategy for leadership is the very life of God Himself. In His "trinity of love and power" there is surrender of individualism without loss of identity, and subordination of will without inferiority of status. Since Bethlehem it can never be "beneath me" to "come under" someone else. This is the greatest incentive we need to enter into the joy of shared leadership and – if we are already enjoying it – the greatest incentive to keep it. Maintain this subtle unity and God has a blessing commanded for us. It's something worth guarding at any cost. After all, Gilbert and Sullivan fell out over a carpet and never spoke to one another again!

Notes

1. Derek Kidner, *A Time to Mourn and Time to Dance* (Nottingham; IVP, 1976), p.50.
2. Charles Blair, *The Man Who Could Do No Wrong* (London: Hodder & Stoughton, 1982), p.232.

CHAPTER ELEVEN

Without Fear or Favour

On my first trip to Israel I was privileged to visit the splendid Museum of the Diaspora in Tel Aviv. On the wall of a section devoted to the Jewish community's government of its affairs I found inscribed this word of wisdom, attributed to Rabbi Israel Salanter. "A rabbi whose community does not disagree with him is not really a rabbi; and a rabbi who fears his community is not really a man."

The relationship between leader and people is rarely very simple. Its complexities cannot easily be analysed. But one thing is clear; this relationship makes great demands upon a leader's emotional and psychological resources. The leader is called to a variety of responses as befits the needs of his people and the immediate pressure of God. Paul's emotional agility is a gift from God. "To the Jews I became a Jew, to those without the law as without law ... to the weak I became weak." Timothy was urged to be equally sensitive in his relationships, for the tone and stance appropriate to one person is inappropriate to another (1 Tim. 5:1). This flexibility in response takes time and maturity to achieve if we ever do. Too often this healthy emotional growth is stifled at the outset of one's leadership.

My experience as a minister in a mainline non-conformist denomination confirmed this. I would like to think this only happens in churches where congregational-type forms of church government are in operation, though having observed leaders from other traditions I doubt it. On entering the pastorate of such churches new leaders can find themselves without choice, enmeshed in a whole web of expectations. Leadership attitudes are in part programmed in advance by the concept of ministry such leadership is working under. It is assumed that the minister, pastor, vicar or team-leader will act as a figurehead to whatever organisations they have inherited, irrespective of their value. It is expected of them without question that they will play certain well-defined traditional roles in the ecclesiastical game. Independence of action and reaction is severely curtailed and the range of possible pastoral initiatives narrowed down by a quickly acquired sense of the people's assent or disapproval. The leader's role rapidly becomes *typecast* and often stilted and stereotyped in its personal humanity.

All this may be subtly and fatally reinforced by an economic dependence on the people for his stipend and clergy house. To notice this is not sour grapes, nor is it to question the sincerity of those who operate the system. Still less does it imply that all pastors are cowards. Yet even raising these kind of issues in ministers' fraternals once brought wrath down on my head. Much of this is an understandable defensive reaction. Things have improved considerably I have no doubt. But the question of where a leader derives emotional security from is one that needs to be faced. A leader voted in, can be voted out, not always for godly reasons. Hired on flimsy evidence, a leader can be fired for even less. Not that being popular is proof against the process I am describing. We all like to be liked. When all speak well of us is may be just the time when we need to examine the basis of our emotional security. For the situation I have outlined is a recipe for caution and conserving the status quo. Only those of a strong prophetic spirit and a certain emotional detachment avoid succumbing to it.

It is heartening to realise that Jesus faced both popularity and hostility and treated those two imposters just the same. "They got up, drove him out of the town, and took him to the brow of the hill on which the town was built, in order to throw him down the cliff. But he walked right through the crowd and went on his way" (Luke 4:29). "After the people saw the miraculous sign that Jesus did, they began to say, 'Surely this is the Prophet who is to come into the world.' Jesus, knowing that they intended to come and make him king by force, withdrew again to a mountain by himself" (John 6:14–15). No one is suggesting a fate or a temptation anything like as grand for us as for Him. Our crosses and our carrots are altogether on a much more minor scale. But then our resistance is so much lower than His that we need to keep Him in our sights. Secure in His Father's love and calling, satisfied with nothing less than the Father's joy and reward, He cut through the web of other people's enforced expectations. They had not paid Him to be the Piper and so could not call His tune. There was no threat that could deter Him and no inducement divert Him from His

Father's will. At this point it is good to ask a question or two about my emotional well-being as a leader of God's people.

Am I motivated to lead by my own emotional insecurity?

The danger here is that leadership meets too great a psychological need in my life than is good for my integrity in ministry. A survey by a clinical psychologist of over 50 of America's top comedians found that most of them were sad and depressed men. Their comedy performances were an outlet for their rage and anxiety. What kept them going psychologically was the love and laughter of the audience. Similar pitfalls and pressures face all those in spiritual ministry.[1] As A.W. Tozer pointed out, "The free man has never been a religious tyrant, nor has he lorded it over God's heritage. It is fear and lack of self-assurance that has led men to try to crush others under their feet."[2] Every one of us has emotional deficiencies of some kind, but it is probably wise not to appoint as leaders those who have serious psychological problems. This may be one reason for Paul's warning about appointing recent converts to positions of responsibility within the Church. The overseer "must not be a recent convert, or he may become conceited ..." (1 Tim. 3:6). Every one of us was a newcomer to leadership at some time or another and we must make allowances if budding leaders are to develop. But in the current trend among newly planted churches towards greater freedom and naturalness in public ministry and meetings I have noticed a constant fault among emerging leaders. In an effort to be relaxed and natural with the people, they have become slovenly in style and expression. They often behave in a "jokey" and self-conscious way that makes others embarrassed. Churches deserve better than to have immaturity foisted on them under the guise of greater informality.

Scrambled ego

Even those of us who are neither neurotic nor novices end up in a tangle of emotional reactions from time to time. When, for example, I am afraid to disagree or am annoyed at being disagreed with, the warning signs are there. My zeal to call down fire on those I think my enemies may on reflection turn out like James' and John's outburst to be merely natural hot-headedness (Luke 9:54). My excessive caution when adventurous moves are suggested and my proneness to raise every conceivable obstacle to committing myself to some new initiative may appear to be the height of wisdom and maturity. In fact, like the leader in the parable, I may be burying my talent, venturing nothing because I do not know God well enough to make mistakes, fearing His wrath when I should be trusting His grace (Luke 19:21).

To attempt to "un-mix" our motives is as futile as trying to unscramble an egg. Paul didn't attempt such self-analysis: "I do not even judge myself. My conscience is clear, but that does not make me innocent. It is the Lord who judges me" (1 Cor. 4:4). Unscrambling our mixed-up egos is the Lord's work, for when He comes "he will bring to light what is hidden in darkness and will expose the motives of men's hearts" (1 Cor. 4:5). So the answer to all this is not an obsessive introspection. What I need to do is to repent and to gain God's sense of proportion. I need to get things into perspective again and to renew that purity of heart which seeks God's glory above all else.

Am I governed by fear in attempts to be a leader?

Newcomers are especially vulnerable here. Joshua feels it when faced with the task of succeeding Moses in the leadership of Israel. Timothy feels it when given responsibility by Paul, his "spiritual father". "Be strong and very courageous" Joshua is urged. "Fear not" seems a recurring exhortation in God's instruction manual for leaders. Isaiah is called not to fear what the people fear (Isa. 8:12). Jeremiah was commanded: "Do not be afraid of them, for I am with you and will rescue you" (Jer. 1:8). To fear men here would only plunge the prophet into deeper doubt. "Do not be terrified by them or I will terrify you before them" is what the prophet hears and it cuts off his escape route immediately. The Lord is quick to add by way of reassurance: "Today I have made you a fortified city ... They will fight against you but will not overcome you" (Jer. 1:18–19). "Do not be afraid of them or their words" is the encouragement Ezekiel receives (Ezek. 2:6). In a vision Paul is told: "Do not be afraid; keep on speaking, do not be silent" as he faces the daunting task of evangelising pagan Corinth (Acts 18:9).

Inferiority and inadequacy can make us emotional cripples.

"I'm not young enough" (Abraham).
"I'm not eloquent enough" (Moses).
"I'm not old enough" (Jeremiah).

These can be our first reactions when faced with God's call to lead. Abraham is told not to limit the possibilities open to God, Moses is given a partner to be his spokesman. Timothy is told to let no man "despise his youth", nor to bury his talent in the field of defeatism and inferiority but to dig it up and use it! "For God did not give us a spirit of timidity, but a spirit of power, of love and of self-discipline" (2 Tim. 1:7).

The task of restoring order and truth to the Church of God is hard enough in our day for us to be able to identify with Nehemiah. Faced with fierce antagonism and opposition to the work of reconstruction to which he is called, he sees clearly what is happening. "They were all trying to frighten us, thinking, 'Their hands will get too weak for the work, and it will not be completed.' But I prayed, 'Now strengthen my hands' " (Neh. 6:9).

I recall an incident many years ago when the church of which I was pastor was at a crucial and early stage of renewal. Not everything I was teaching or seeking to do was proving acceptable to everyone. Hostility to me as the leader was increasing. One lady wrote me a very bitter and accusing letter. My father was staying with us at the time and he knew what to do. "Let's bring this to the Lord, son"; and we did, spreading the letter out on the bed as we knelt beside it. We prayed that the Lord would strengthen my hands so that I might not be deterred by fear from going through with the changes the Holy Spirit was calling us to. Later I realised there was good scriptural precedent for this in the life of Hezekiah. Receiving a hostile and accusing letter from Rabshakah, I read, "Hezekiah spread it out before the Lord" asking the Lord to deal with it and the opposition it expressed (Isa. 37:14). What the Lord did for Hezekiah He did in fact do for me if less dramatically. The lady left for a new postal district! Out of this experience and others like it later I was able to encourage another pastor who was also being used of God to bring change to the Church. He too was being unjustly and bitterly misrepresented and resisted by some members of his church. I gave him a slip of paper. Written on it were two lines of a hymn by Charles Wesley which I had recently taken to heart.

Shall I for fear of feeble men
The Spirit's course in me restrain?

If nothing else it gave me, as I hope it did him, a wholesome sense of perspective and helped me laugh at myself and my fears.

As the wise man saw, "the fear of man will prove to be a snare" (Prov. 29:25). The escape for leaders here as elsewhere is that "fear of the Lord which is the beginning of wisdom" and the start of an emotional stability in their relationship with the people they are called to lead. The fear of the Lord frees me as a leader from the anxious need to defend or vindicate myself. The love of the Father frees me to challenge people's assumptions and to break the mould even at the risk of their misunderstanding. The leader who grows towards this end will stay genuine and avoid the typecasting that can destroy one's integrity.

Notes

1. For an interesting assessment of the state of mind of a representative selection of evangelical ministers in the UK, see *Pastoral Care Today; practice, problems and priorities in churches today* – a professional survey initiated by CWR in conjunction with the Evangelical Alliance and conducted by Rev Professor Leslie Francis, Rev Dr William Kay and Ms Mandy Robbins at the Centre for Ministry Studies, University of Wales, Bangor, which was published in 2000. An additional report under the same auspices and with the same data on the personality profiles of people in ministry is also available from CWR.
2. A.W. Tozer, *Of God and Men* (Harrisburg: Christian Publications, 1960), pp.15–16.

CHAPTER TWELVE

Alarm Bells for Leaders

Every leader has his weak spot! Graffiti scrawled on a wall in Canterbury during the saintly Dr Coggan's reign as Archbishop and Primate of all England, accused: "Dr Coggan cheats at Scrabble." Were this all we had to worry us as leaders we could rest easy but unfortunately it isn't. Leaders are in the frontline of the spiritual battle. Often they are among its first victims. Leaders are exposed to pressures and temptations beyond the usual run of testing. Pitfalls face the unwary and traps abound even for the experienced. "We all stumble in many ways" as the apostle James observed. For this reason the apostolic advice is clear: "Not many of you should presume to be teachers, my brothers, because you know that we who teach will be judged more strictly" (James 3:1).

Charles Blair's story is a salutary one. Pastor of one of the biggest churches in America, his drive and ambition led him and his people into debt and litigation. Found guilty of the fraudulent sale of securities, Dr Blair faced total humiliation. His realism and honesty in accepting responsibility and his subsequent restoration make for moving reading. "Alarm bells should have rung," he admits, "when they called me the 'man who could do no wrong'." [1]

"Take heed to yourself and your ministry" was more than once Paul's word of warning. "Watch your life closely, keep a grip on your life's purpose, concentrate on your ministry" – these bring out the flavour of his apostolic injunctions (Acts 20:28; 1 Tim. 4:16). The misgivings about leadership that have been hinted at so far in this book have now huddled together in this chapter and we need to look at them in order to be on our guard against them. Mistakes can be avoided if leaders will only ask themselves the right questions.

(i) *Am I over-concerned with image building?*
Am I more ready to believe what people say about me than what I know God says about me? Am I becoming less able to cope with their appreciation, turning their praise into flattery which feeds my vanity?

Paul needed a deliverance from the people before he could safely minister to them (Acts 26:17)! Professionalism is the greatest danger here, forming a protective shield behind which we may cherish all kinds of inflated ideas of our own importance. Have I become adept at deflecting just criticism by pulling rank or manipulating the situation to put myself in a good light? To have no guile here is to be really blessed. Over-exposure to spiritual things can breed unreality unless we are living in the good of them. Fenelon once pointed out that reading about extraordinary matters can stimulate our imagination to the point where self-love flatters itself that it has attained the attitudes it admires in the books.

(ii) *Am I a member of the Body of Christ?*
Not before time, it has been said, "the clergy are joining the Church!" This is good news, for the very leaders most concerned about the "fringers" have often been one of them. When I was a student it was received ministerial wisdom for the pastor not to have any close friends in the church. Doubtless many still believe it as they eke out their lives in loneliness. Leaders who can't be ministered to by the people they are serving lose, as Peter was in danger of doing, a large and personal share of Jesus in His Body (John 13:8). Having overcome the fear of being taken advantage of, my wife and I enjoyed and depended on the prayers, support and friendship of the members of the church of which I was pastor for 13 years.

(iii) *Do I have a growing awareness of the extent of my gift and ministry?*
Am I moving easily within what God has called me to be? Leaders needs to know their limitation, their measure and their sphere.

(a) They need to know the *limitation of their gift*. When Peter said "not the cross, Lord" he was falling into the trap of knowing better than the Lord, of presuming to dictate to Him what should and should not happen. But to do this is to fail to recognise the limits of one's gift and is to forget that each of us has a God-given responsibility to bear which need not burden us.

(b) They need to know their *measure of faith*. Peter failed here in becoming over-confident, in thinking that his loyalty was beyond question. This is precisely where we need to take heed to ourselves as leaders. With each gift comes "a measure of faith" (Rom. 12:3ff.). It may be enlarged but is sufficient for the task in hand. To go beyond it involves us in dangerous presumption; to stay within it brings joy to us and benefit to the Body of Christ.

(c) They need to know their *sphere of service*. Peter in his enthusiasm was tempted to assume responsibility which God was not giving him. But he was told that it was none of his business what another man was given to do. Paul wanted to re-assure the Corinthians about himself and his team that "We, however, will not boast beyond proper limits, but will confine our boasting to the field God has assigned to us" (2 Cor. 10:12–18). In fact our authority has greater weight, Paul says, because "we are not over-extending ourselves". Pressed to undertake commitments on every side, today's leaders would do well to take this to heart. Knowing our limitations is a saving grace. When Thomas Buckley ran for the post of auditor of Massachusetts in 1941, his speech is said to have consisted of just seven words: "I am an auditor, not an orator!" He won. It may never be as cut-and-dried as this for leadership teams seeking to follow the Spirit into an always expanding ministry. But Paul at least did not seem abashed at regularly defining who and what he was.

Character and charisma

(iv) *Have I a healthy determination to maintain integrity?*
Many of the great "healers" of the 1950s in America came to a sad end. Some died young, others took to drink or drugs, still others took early retirement and live out their lives in obscurity. With such immense gifts amidst a supernatural outpouring it is tempting to ask what went wrong. Before we judge such men too harshly we need to appreciate the tremendous pressures such a ministry put them under. Clearly in too many cases these men overloaded their systems, living beyond their emotional, spiritual and moral resources. Their charisma outstripped their characters. Character weaknesses were overlooked in the glamour and pressure of the ministry of the miraculous. The fact that God in His infinite mercy did not withhold His power or His

anointing led many to the wrong conclusion that miracles justified immorality. Uncritical self-assessment bolstered by unquestioning adulation held reality at bay. Deception was not far away. It was not long before many of these greatly gifted servants of God felt themselves to be above normal standards and criteria, operating to a different law of righteousness from everyone else, not answerable or accountable as others were for their inconsistencies and lack of integrity. The way to avoid this slippery slope is by an honest facing and confessing of our weaknesses and mistakes, consistent willingness to "judge ourselves that we be not judged", and a commitment to "seek first the kingdom of God and his righteousness".

Asking "Why?"

(v) *Am I prepared to ask awkward questions of my own leadership?*
Comparison with the temptations of the Lord Jesus will help to underline this need to scrutinise our motives closely. Jesus was first tempted to *prove* His Sonship by performing miracles. Like Him we do not need to prove ourselves to Father in this way. But insecurity at this point will cause us to strive too hard for success. Like the compulsive worker described by Solomon, we may succumb to activism, never asking "For whom am I toiling?" (Eccl. 4:8). Zeal without knowledge was a feature of the worst kind of Pharisaism. The problem in this is a failure to ask "Why?"; why am I doing this? why am I going there? Asking the question will at least keep us on our toes, help to cleanse us of egotism and revive in us an exclusive concern for God and His glory.

Asking "How?"

Jesus was next tempted to *presume* on His Sonship to do a startling but needless act. The danger of presumption is ever-present, especially for those called to an adventurous ministry of faith. Moses strikes the rock to produce water on one occasion and then presumes quite wrongly that this is to be God's method on a later occasion. Once before he had confused carnal zeal with spiritual boldness when he mistakenly "thought that his own people would realise that God was using him to rescue them ..." (Acts 7:25). This is to confuse self-will with God's will. It is to have a God-given idea but to make wrong assumptions about the methods God wants to employ. The question to ask is the one Mary asked: "*How*, Lord?" God's ends do not justify our means. We need to ask Him how He wants us to act or to approach a matter, as David was wise enough to do (2 Sam. 5).

Asking "When?"

Jesus was also tempted to *pre-empt* the gains of the cross by accepting the kingdoms of this world from the hands of the devil. Abraham tried to speed up the fulfilment of God's promise and got Ishmael for his pains. Impatience is often our greatest danger. We want a short-term success at the expense of God's long-term will. We override scruples and misgivings in an attempt to be giants of faith. We put our faith in faith, claim more than we can honestly provide evidence for, exaggerate the effects of our work – all in a desire to accelerate the hand of God. This is sheer presumption. It shows a consistent unwillingness to ask the crucial question "*When?*" To seek to know God's timing is especially the need of those with prophetic vision who otherwise might seek to hasten and thus distort God's programme (1 Pet. 1:10; cf. 1 Tim. 5:22). In any case pastoral ministry is long-haul work, calling for a "long obedience in the same direction".

Asking "*why?*", "*how?*" and "*when?*" then is the kind of self-scrutiny that will help us avoid many pitfalls. Of the others, two are perhaps quite obvious but worth mentioning for that reason.

(vi) *Am I becoming authoritarian?*
One sign of this in a leader is to be become over-defensive in the face of criticism. Do I find it difficult to hear any criticism of the work without becoming resentful. And what of our attitude to those in our care? A pastoral leader can sometimes degenerate into a mere "busybody" anxious to put other people right. At worst, like Rehoboam who forsook the wisdom of his father Solomon, a leader can become overbearing and harsh. Ignoring the advice of the more experienced elders who assured the new king that he would win the hearts of the people if he was willing to serve them, Rehoboam listened instead to the counsel of hotheaded younger men who urged him to assert his authority and make the yoke of the people heavier not lighter (1 Kings

12:1–11). This domineering spirit is one we need to guard against. We are called to shepherd the flock of God "not lording it over" those entrusted to us (1 Pet. 5:3).

There is one final question that needs asking.

(vii) *Am I serving the Lord or His house?*
The distinction is made by the prophet Ezekiel who tells us that the sons of Zadok were rewarded for their faithfulness by being called to minister directly to the Lord while others merely served the sanctuary (Ezek. 44:15f.). Neglecting our personal ministry to the Lord is a perennial danger for leaders. It was partly to offset this that the apostles involved others in the work of administration so that they could devote their full attention to the ministry of the Word and prayer. Jesus told a pertinent parable about this. After a long hard day in the fields, a servant arrives home to be told by his master: "Prepare my supper, get yourself ready and wait on me" (Luke 17:8). Beyond all the tiring and necessary work demanded of us in His service, we are also called to minister to the Master's own personal satisfaction. To worship Him, to love Him, to wait upon Him, is a leader's greatest safeguard as well as his greatest refreshment. The question the Chief Shepherd most wants His under-shepherds to answer is not "Do you know more than these or do more than these?" It is "Do you love me more than these?" Before we leave the subject and to do justice to the apostle Peter, we take note of F.F. Bruce's verdict on him. "Peter had it in him to be a stone of stumbling or a foundation stone. Thanks to the intercession which his master had made for him in a critical hour, he strengthened his brethren and became a rock of stability and a focus of unity."[2]

Notes

1. Charles Blair, *The Man Who Could Do No Wrong* (London: Hodder & Stoughton, 1982), p.232.
2. F.F. Bruce, *Men and Movements in Primitive Christianity* (Exeter; Paternoster, 1979), p.48.

CHAPTER THIRTEEN

Watergate in the Church

Apart from having no leadership at all, the next worse thing that can befall any community of God's people is to have bad leadership. Ever since Nadab and Abihu, there have been those only too ready to offer strange fire on the altar of God's service by taking matters into their own hands. Ever since Uzzah steadied the ark, shrewd operators have tried to balance things up as if they knew better than God. Some have been simply misguided, a few openly cynical, but phonies, charlatans and hirelings have climbed over the wall of God's fold all too often.

According to the prophet Isaiah, one way in which God exercises judgement on His people is by removing their established leaders altogether (Isa. 3:1–12). The ensuing vacuum is quickly filled by opportunists, by the inexperienced and immature, by capricious and incompetent youths, by women acting as men or, worse, by men acting as women! "I will make boys their officials; mere children will govern them" (Isa.3:4). No longer are there true leaders, only *mis*leaders! (cf. Isa. 3:12). Leadership goes begging, standards fall, desperation sets in until "anybody will do" (cf. Isa. 3:6–7). The reluctant are press-ganged into leadership and arm-twisting replaces the call of God.

This is serious if for no other reason than that a people's prosperity is measured by its priests, its level of life by its standard of leadership. The prophets plainly laid the responsibility for Israel's declension at the door of its official leaders. Prophets who prophesy falsely, priests who lack knowledge, kings who rule unjustly, shepherds who pull the wool over everyone's eyes – all feel the impact of the prophetic indictment (Jer. 2:8; Ezek. 22:6). Where renewal is needed it starts with repentant leaders (Joel 2:17).

The resurgence of interest in spiritual leadership in recent decades has been a welcome development. In Britain, at least, the Church for too long suffered from a generation of false leaders who sold out to the theological bankruptcy of liberalism. Having repudiated the supernatural in favour of philosophy, having torn up an infallible Bible, these "shepherds" scattered the flock and destroyed its faith. Now God has been raising up a new generation of leaders at every level of the Church's life to be the leaven in the lump. But so important is it to guard the flock of God from its hireling shepherds, that we must note the marks of false leadership. Jeremiah 8 is a prophetic place to start.

False leaders are not necessarily innovators but may mislead by their unquestioning trust in accepted tradition. Complacently going by the book, they may fail to realise how badly they are confusing God's will with men's wisdom (Jer. 8:8–9). They are the "blind leading the blind" which, with an appropriate religious veneer, becomes the "bland leading the bland". "Shadow boxing" Paul called it; "going through the motions" might be his description now. Every leader must fear the onset of this disease. Constant contact with the living God is the only safeguard against it.

False leaders are mere professionals. If few are in it for the money – so poorly paid has the Church's traditional ministry been – the temptation still confronts men in various forms (Jer. 8:10). When the role outstrips the emotional security we have, then keeping our status may become subtly but surely too important to us. This is to feed ourselves rather than the sheep and is to run the gauntlet of Ezekiel's protest (Ezek. 34:2,8).

One recurrent feature of leaders who lack integrity and truth is that *they pander to the people.* Speaking to please the people, telling their hearers what they want to hear, false prophets bring superficial healing to the Church's deep wounds. Afraid to be unpopular, such leaders lull their followers into a false sense of complacency before God (8:11). Ezekiel calls this "smearing whitewash". Speaking "pleasant things" and "illusions" is how Isaiah describes it (Isa. 30:10). Paul warned Timothy of the time coming when men, tiring of "sound doctrine" and "to suit their own desires", will "gather around them a great number of teachers to say what their itching ears want to hear" (2 Tim. 4:3). The true prophet of God will not be misled by receiving appreciation for his style at the expense of adherence to his word (Ezek. 33:30–33). And the true son of the prophets among the messengers of Jesus will be uneasy when too many speak too well of him (Luke 6:26) "for in the same way their fathers used to treat the false prophets".

This sensitivity to God and His truth is lacking in the false leaders. According to Jeremiah he is *shameless in his contribution to the scandal he is part of*. He does not "even know how to blush" (Jer. 8:12). He feels no pain at the reproach God's people bear. He is impervious to the embarrassment God feels at His people's disgrace. But the true leader is grieved that God's advertisement in the world is so poor a representation of Him. "Let the priests, who minister before the Lord, weep … Let them say: 'Spare your people, O Lord. Do not make your inheritance an object of scorn, a byword among the nations' " (Joel 2:17). And they do this not because denominational statistics are in a nose-dive but because the world has stopped even asking "Where is your God?"

In fact we may be in gravest danger when we become paranoid about the Church's survival and deem it our duty to do anything to perpetuate the Church. But desperate times do not demand desperate measures, only renewed and godly ones. Being seeker-friendly is one thing: making the gospel user-friendly is quite another.

Nor are we evangelicals and charismatics immune. Although we are not liable to fall for the latest "myth of God incarnate" heresy, we are liable to hook the complete red-herring. We are prone to ride every wind of unusual doctrine and surf every fashionable wave of experience for fear of not being spiritually "with it". Since this book was first written the charismatic church has fallen for some feeble fads! But prophets who prophesy falsely are if anything more dangerous than false prophets; we are more easily taken in by them.

"The false prophet", in John Oman's classic definition, "is a shell gathering up and echoing the temper of the age; the true prophet is no echo of the moods and passions of the age but a living voice declaring what is its true lesson."[1]

Many years ago I heard this wise word of prophecy given.

I do not want you to be men who collect things from other men like Aaron.

I want you to go up the mountain yourselves.

I want you to be men of *the first phase not the second phase*.

You are to be men of integrity even above human friendship and to press on with me.

You are to come down and be angry if need be with the people, not popular; otherwise you will produce a copy of something seen long ago.

I will lead my people through men who have been in my presence.

I will speak and engrave it in your hearts.

You will see things. Be impatient for this, to see things.

Be discontented, not satisfied with a collection of gold from other men.

For what I say and do will be eternal.

As a prophecy it was just for us: but as a prayer I share it with you. Pray it with me and keep strange fire off God's altars.

Notes

1. John Oman, *Grace and Personality* (London: Collins, 1917/1962), p.21.

CHAPTER FOURTEEN

Checkpoint

It's time for a check-up to see if the story so far is our story.

(i) Am I using the *ability* God has given me?
In fact, what is my basic gift? What other gifts do I desire in order to serve the Lord better? Do I need to stir up the gifts I have to fulfil my potential?

(ii) What is my *ambition* as a servant of God?
Are my aspirations godly desires or private fantasies? Am I "seeking great things" for myself or am I wanting to do more with a view to glorifying God?

(iii) Have I an *anointing* for what I am doing?
Do I need the Holy Spirit to do it or not? Am I relying on the resources and energies of the Spirit or getting by on my own? Am I eking out my strength in Christian ministry or am I "always abounding in the work of the Lord"?

(iv) Is my ministry by divine *appointment*?
Am I pushy or an opportunist or do I have a genuine calling in God? Have I the deep unrest that comes from attempting to be a self-made ministry or do I have the peace which comes from working within the scope of my calling?

(v) Who gave me *authority* to do what I am doing?
Do I submit to the authority of the Word of God by being a doer of it as well as a hearer of it? What is the impact of my life (what I am), my calling (what my role is) and my function (what I can do)? Am I under the authority of any other man or men of God?

(vi) Does my ministry find its *authentication* in my life?
Do my actions speak differently to my words? Does my character match my charisma? By my fruits am I known as a credible representative of Jesus? Do I have moral authority as well as spiritual authority?

(vii) Do I enjoy the *approval* of God in what I am doing?

Is there an ease and a grace about what I am doing? Am I serving the Lord with a sense of freedom that promotes faith and a sense of mastery that produces confidence in others? Am I always struggling to do the job or do I relish tackling the tasks my calling brings?

(viii) Have I the *assurance* which enables me to serve without striving?

Am I manipulating people or events to put myself in a good light or to make myself needed? Am I aware of a competitive spirit that jostles for position or status? Am I beginning to need praise and appreciation out of emotional insecurity? Do I enjoy the praise which comes from integrity and the immunity from fear which a good conscience provides?

(ix) Do I accept the principle of *accountability*?

To whom am I responsible for my ministry? Am I willing to answer for my results? Is there anyone I can go to for help and honest advice? Is there one other person I can trust to know the worst about me who will love me just the same?

(x) Can others count on my *availability*?

In replying to tributes made to him on the occasion of his eightieth birthday, Karl Barth reminded his friends that a donkey once had the privilege of being allowed to carry Jesus to Jerusalem. He went on:

> If I have done anything in my life, I have done it as a relative of the donkey that went its way carrying an important burden. The disciples had said to its owner "The Lord has need of it." And so it seems to have pleased God to have used me at this time, just as I was, in spite of all the things, the disagreeable things, that quite rightly are and will be said about me. Thus I was used. That is how I happened to be present and that was my work. I just happened to be on the spot.[1]

Notes

1. Karl Barth, *Fragments Grave and Gay* (London: Collins, 1971), pp.116–117.

Part Three
Follow My Leader

CHAPTER FIFTEEN

Jesus: His Clash with Leadership

In the United Kingdom, unlike the United States, a change of government does not bring a change in the Civil Service. The permanent staff who keep the machinery of government going can stay at their posts even when an election puts another political party in office. This makes for great stability. Unfortunately, it is also a major barrier to change. Friction between the permanent officials and ministers of the incoming government is frequent, especially when more radical political parties assume office.

When Jesus appeared with the radical impact of the government of God, He threatened the ruling establishment of His day. Between Him and the religious civil servants He met there was inevitable conflict. He clashed with the guardians of the legislature who had obscured God's pure law with the small print of manmade regulations and by-laws. The trustees of tradition and the custodians of the Temple and its treasury both found Him too prophetic to accommodate. Hawkish Pharisees, liberal Sadducees, middle-of-the-road scribes, extremist Zealots with their "extra-parliamentary" methods – all found Him too different to fit into their category or group. To them all He was a provocation. Small wonder He so consistently predicted that His death would be at the hands of the "chief priests, and scribes and Pharisees". This was no accident but part of God's plan to remove a decadent leadership and to raise up a new leadership for the people of God.

Matthew, our "civil servant" evangelist, shows us that the clash started at the earliest possible stage. When the magi asked Herod "Where is he who has been born king of the Jews?" he was "disturbed, and all Jerusalem with him" (Matt. 2:3). Herod's "think tank" then correctly identified Jesus' birthplace as Bethlehem by tracing the source of this threat to their kingdom to the prophecy of Micah. "But you, Bethlehem Ephrathah, though you are small among the clans of Judah, out of you will come for me one who will be ruler over Israel" (Micah 5:2). Herod's brutal and indiscriminate massacre of the innocents in the Bethlehem area shows just how afraid he was that this shepherd-ruler might materialise to destroy his already crumbling power-base. What was prophetically certain is that it would involve the unmasking of false authority and the unveiling of true authority. The shepherd-ruler would be a breaker of the old and a maker of the new. "I will bring them together like sheep in a pen, like a flock in its pasture; the place will throng with people. One who *breaks open the way* will go up before them" (Micah 2:12–13, my emphasis).

Lords of misrule

In Matthew 23 there is an unmasking by Jesus of the false authority He confronted. He does not advocate a coup d'état to overthrow the teaching of the Pharisees but shows up the sham in their behaviour. He exposes them as leaders who fail to practise what they preach (v.3), who offload responsibility onto others less able to bear it (v.4), who are publicity conscious and blatantly concerned for their professional image (v.5), who are status seekers and status keepers (vv.6–7). Such leaders close down rather than open up the kingdom to men (v.13). They exploit the vulnerable and perpetuate their own errors in the converts they make (vv.14–15). They are legalists who have lost all sense of perspective, unable now to see the wood for the trees (vv.23–24). They turn truth inside out and upside down while pretending to be its defenders (vv.25–28). They show a phony reverence for the past, claiming to be the heirs of the very men their forefathers murdered (vv.29ff.)!

Jesus, for His part, is training a new leadership for God's people. Onto this scene of misrule He plans to send His own representatives and delegated authorities: "Therefore, I am sending you prophets and wise men and teachers" (Matt. 23.34). Their brutal rejection by the existing leaders of Israel will be the indictment and the undoing of all the false leaders of God's people. The calling of the Twelve by Jesus was more than a mere pragmatic action reinforcing our earlier lessons on plurality among leaders. It was a key strategic decision. By choosing twelve men Jesus was serving notice of His intention to raise up a Messianic ministry and leadership among God's people. John Yoder was a pioneer of the recent recognition of Jesus as a profoundly political figure. In his words, "New teachings are no threat, as long as the teacher stands alone: a movement, extending his personality in both time and space, presenting an alternative to the structures that were there before, challenges the system as no mere words ever could."[1]

It is a simplistic error to say that the Church has replaced Israel just as it is a literalistic error to say that Israel and the Church are to remain for ever two separate entities. Better to say that through the death and resurrection of her Messiah, Israel is *being reconstituted* as the called-out people of God in a Church which includes Jew and Gentile on equal terms. Over this final "one flock" there will be one Shepherd with His twelve appointed under-shepherds as co-leaders with Him. " 'I tell you the truth, at the renewal of all things, when the Son of Man sits on his glorious throne, you who have followed me will also sit on twelve thrones, judging the twelve tribes of Israel' " (Matt. 19:28). Meanwhile, as we saw at the outset of this book, the style of His leadership is in sharp contrast to the corrupt leadership it supplants. " 'You are not to be called "Rabbi", for you have only one Master ... And do not call anyone on earth "father", for you have one Father ... Nor are you to be called "teacher", for you have one Teacher, the Christ' " (Matt. 23:8–10). His "lords" are all brothers, His shepherds are also sheep, His teachers are themselves disciples, His leaders are followers, His rulers servants.

In Matthew 15 and 16 the contrast and the clash between true and false authority is clearly drawn. Here Jesus accuses the religious leaders of His day of exalting their tradition over the express commands of God. For the sake of this tradition, He says, they "nullify the word of God" (Matt. 15:6). Emptiness in worship and hollowness in praise are to be traced to a slavish adherence to the precepts of men (15:8–9). Leaders need always to give sound reasons to people for their obedience. Unless we tell them "why" they are to do certain things, we are breeding another tradition. Doing it merely because the leaders say so is the beginning of institutionalism (cf. Isa. 29:13). These leaders which Father has not planted will be uprooted; these blind men vainly seeking to lead a blind people will bring about their own downfall.

Rock against the drift

In the midst of this crumbling foundation Jesus will place a rock and on it build His Church (Matt. 16:18). The era of Messianic leadership is being inaugurated when "a king will reign in righteousness and rulers will rule with justice" (Isa. 32:1f.). In desert conditions sand storms are the enemy of life. The wind whips up the sand never allowing it to settle for life to develop. Barrenness prevails. The rain brings fertility to the unlikeliest places and plants begin to spring up. But it doesn't last. Blasted by the wind, the sand drifts and the fragile vegetation is swept away. But a rock makes all the difference. After rain, in the lee of such a rock, shoots begin to show. Sheltered from the drift, plants have a chance to root and grow. Messiah's leaders are like this. "Each man will be like a shelter from the wind and a refuge from the storm, like streams of water in the desert and the shadow of a great rock in a thirsty land" (Isa. 32:2). This is Peter's calling initially. He is not the dogged defender of the traditions of men but the bold proclaimer of the mysteries of heaven. Entrusted with the Father's revelation of His Son Jesus, he will be anchor man for the Early Church. Like the leading bird in the V-formation of the flock he will bear the brunt of the headwinds. In his apostolic succession all anointed leaders stand.

As a refuge from the wind they will protect the fatherless and widows. As a rock against the drift such Christlike ministry will shelter the Church from error and heresy and every force of anti-Christ. As gullies in the foot of the rock retain the precious water where elsewhere it has evaporated they will be a source of life and faith and hope to the people they lead. As a shade from the sun they will take the pressure off the weak and vulnerable, and give them a chance to grow and develop. Jesus is pledged to base His Church on such ministry.

Leaders with the keys of the kingdom implement heaven's will on earth and move in righteousness and peace. Replacing leaders who have taken away the key of knowledge, they bring God's people into clarity and truth. Such leaders create the conditions for growth. The blind now see because they are led by men and women of vision; the wayward receive clear direction; the confused understand as if for the first time; the incoherent speak clearly and with one voice. Fools have their day of reckoning and true spiritual judgement and discernment restore right values to the Church. Foolish talk is stopped, ungodly attitudes are rooted out, and manipulative scheming is eradicated. No longer are their 57 varieties of opinion plaguing the Church because there is now an honourable person making "noble plans" and practising "noble deeds" in which all the people are secure (Isa. 32:3–8). Such leaders create the conditions for great growth.

Workers for the harvest

"When he saw the crowds, he had compassion on them, because they were harassed and helpless, like sheep without a shepherd" (Matt. 9:36). Jesus felt the misrule keenly because He saw the devastating effects of it in people's lives. The ultimate argument for good leadership is neither pragmatic nor even strategic but pastoral. Suffering people need sensitive shepherds. The Lord Jesus out of His great compassion aims to provide them.

Calling twelve men He delegates to them His own authority to cast out demons and to heal the sick (Matt. 10:1f.). Travelling light, they are to preach what He preached and do what He did! Their coming would prove crucial for every community they visited (10:11ff.). Shepherds though they may be, they are made of the same stuff as their sheep and suffer accordingly (10:16). In their very vulnerability they will prove the presence and power of the Holy Spirit (10:18ff.). To receive them is to receive Christ Himself (10:40ff.), so closely does He identify Himself with them. Going first to the lost sheep of the house of Israel, they are to have the many sheep not of this fold in view. He was training leaders with the multitudes in mind. The false shepherds have fed themselves rather than the sheep. The scribes and Pharisees have failed to strengthen the weak or bind up the broken. They have not sought the lost but have dominated the people, ruling with force and severity (Ezek. 34:1–4). His leaders, by contrast, will "tend the lambs and feed the sheep", not because they have to but because they want to, "not greedy for money, but eager to serve; not lording it over those entrusted to you, but being examples to the flock" (1 Pet. 5:2–3).

To them the appearance of the Chief Shepherd will not be a threat but a reward.

Matthew pinpoints the crucial events which see the final unmasking of false authority and the unveiling of true authority. "Then Jesus told them, 'This very night you will all fall away on account of me, for it is written: "I will strike the shepherd, and the sheep of the flock will be scattered." But after I have risen, *I will go ahead of you* into Galilee' " (Matt. 26:31–32, my emphasis). The clash of leadership has come to a head. Even the trainee leaders of the Shepherd-Ruler have to go through the crucible of failure. The intended rock crumbles like soft sand; Peter denies his Lord (26:34ff.). But the Great Shepherd of the sheep through the blood of everlasting covenant is the one who "breaks open the way" (Micah 2:13). He breaks through His enemies, the lords of misrule and the unseen evil powers behind the scene; He breaks through sin and death and going before them into Galilee, He regroups His scattered flock and trainee under-shepherds. The resurrection which raises the Stone rejected by the experts to the head of the house, reinstates the shaky disciple to be the rock on which He will build His Church. Through disciples like this He will gather the lost and bind up the broken, especially reaching out to all those who have been cynically disregarded by the professional leaders of God's people. In this resurrection reunion the wraps are off. As Micah foresaw, "Their king will pass through before them, the Lord at their head" (Micah 2:13). All authority is now safely back in His hands; the ecclesiastical establishment has been deposed, the religious civil servants have been over-ruled and made redundant. Every position of responsibility among God's people is a "situation now vacant". All appointments to leadership are exclusively in His gift and patronage. "And he gave some to be apostles, some to be prophets ..."

Notes

1. John H. Yoder, *The Politics of Jesus* (Grand Rapids: Eerdmans, 1972), p.40.

CHAPTER SIXTEEN

Jesus: His Model for Leadership

It is as a Son apprenticed to His Father's trade that Jesus becomes a model of leadership for us. He is confessing success not failure when He says, "By myself I can nothing" (John 5:30). If we are to follow Him in this we shall have to recognise that we may be too full of our own schemes and ways of doing things to be of immediate use to Him. If we are to be like Him in doing only what we see the Father doing, we shall need to listen more attentively to the Father's voice and be more aware of where the creative Spirit is doing new things. To be a leader like Jesus, God's starting points must be my starting-points. Doing only what we see Father doing will demand a break with the pattern of expectations put upon us as leaders by our particular brand of church-manship, or even by our supposedly charismatic spontaneity.

Following Father like this will certainly free us from rigid preconceived ideas of ministry. Because it was so purposeful, Christ's life was unprogrammed. He did not have a five-year diary! Responsive to His Father's will He was flexible enough to withstand even popular demand in order to move on to the next appointed place. "The people ... tried to keep him from leaving them. But he said, 'I must preach the good news of the kingdom of God to the other towns also, because that is why I was sent' " (Luke 4:42–43). As well as creativity and flexibility, this gave Him great objectivity too. "By myself I can do nothing; I judge only as I hear" (John 5:30). Prisoner of no one's prejudices, in the patronage of no sectarian school, He spoke the truth firsthand from His Father. Any leader who follows the Master in this will be, in some measure, radical and prophetic in thrust and will inevitably disrupt the polite diplomacy and cautious consensus that passes for wisdom in most church circles. Above all, a realisation of sonship brings an immense sense of security. It was out of such a sense of deep security that Jesus felt so free to serve as the lowest slave in washing the feet of His disciples. The thirteenth chapter of John spells out for us the style of leadership on which our own is to be based.

He stoops to conquer

Jesus is secure in knowing who He is and this frees Him to serve. "Jesus knew that the Father had put all things under his power" (John 13:3) – and knowing what He had received from His Father, He knew what He had to give to men. "Jesus knew ... that he had come from God" (v.3) – and knowing where He had come from, He knew what His calling was. "Jesus knew that ... he was returning to God" (v.3) – and knowing where He was going, He knew what His aims and objectives were. "Jesus knew that the time had come for him to leave this world" (v.1) – and knowing the timing of God He knew when to make significant moves in His ministry. Uninhibited by self-consciousness, or by fear of losing face or reputation, He is free to stoop to wash the feet of uncomprehending followers. Secure in being a Son of God, He is able to risk their misunderstanding and to do for them prophetically what only later will they come to thank Him for. He is our example of leadership. Secure in our sonship we will not need to strive for position in order to prove who we are. We will not use our leadership opportunities to find emotional wholeness but to express it. In this security we will be able to lay down our reputation as leaders in order to fulfil our calling. We will be freed to act prophetically at the risk of being misunderstood. We will have no need to waste emotional energy on vindicating ourselves. "For we do not preach ourselves, but Jesus Christ as Lord, and ourselves as your servants for Jesus' sake" (2 Cor. 4:5).

Servant of God

The role of the servant is most clearly drawn out biblically in the so-called "servant songs" of Isaiah's prophecy in chapters 42, 49, 50 and 53. These songs provide a corrective to a too manward and social a view of servanthood. Isaiah's picture is very different. He portrays the servant not as a general factotum but as fulfilling specific tasks and embarked upon a special mission. Furthermore, he is God's servant before he is man's helper. It is God who sets him these tasks and equips him for them. The world neither writes the agenda for the Church nor the work-schedules for the Church's leaders.

The first servant song makes this clear. *The servant-leader is God's man first and foremost*. God chooses him, upholds him, delights in him. As we have seen before it is only God who can adequately equip him. "I will put my Spirit on him and he will bring justice to the nations" (Isa. 42:1). Endorsed by God he is sent out to do God's work and implement His will in the world. A feature of the servant-leader is his remarkable reticence, his distinctive modesty, which means that he does not "shout or cry out, or raise his voice in the streets" (Isa. 42:2). He keeps a provocatively low profile. He does not draw needless attention to himself. One wonders how much at home he would be in that brash side of evangelicalism which is almost a branch of show business. By the same token he might well disdain the over-bearing manner that passes for confidence in some charismatic circles.

The servant-leader is marked by a gentleness which makes him great. "A bruised reed he will not break, and a smouldering wick he will not snuff out" (Isa. 42:3). He is keen to encourage the weak and bolster the confidence of the timid. He will seek to impart faith and hope to the dispirited and to fan into flame potential gifts and abilities in others. Not allowing his own spirit to be broken or his own light to be snuffed out, he maintains an unquenchable optimism and an uncrushable determination. Miraculously, "he will not falter or be discouraged" (Isa. 42:4).

The key to the servant's success is a secret life with God. The second servant song speaks of this. As a sword stays bright in its scabbard and an arrow sharp in its quiver, so the servant maintains his public effectiveness by continuous fellowship with God. In Robert Murray M'Cheyne's now famous words, "Do not forget the culture of the inner man – I mean of the heart. How diligently the cavalry officer keeps his sabre clean and sharp; every stain he rubs off with the greatest care. Remember you are God's sword. A holy minister is an aweful weapon in the hand of God."[1] Even when he feels he has "laboured to no purpose" (Isa. 49:4ff.) he refreshes himself in God and soon finds himself with a renewed and even enlarged mission.

He is a servant also of the Word of God. What he hears in secret he speaks in public. "The Sovereign Lord has given me an instructed tongue, to know the word that sustains the weary. He wakens me morning by morning, wakens my ear to listen like one being taught" (Isa. 50:4). This freshness and immediacy of the Word makes him a source of counsel and makes his words "spirit and … life" (John 6:63). Nourished by the living Word himself he provides daily bread for others. He is able to speak different things to different people according to their needs. Freed from secondhand clichés and stock-in-trade answers, he gives words of wisdom and knowledge appropriate to the occasion. This daily responsiveness to the will of God inevitably brings him to a Gethsemane crisis in which he looks to God for his vindication. The servant-leader, face set like flint, remains nonetheless strangely vulnerable.

To say all this is, of course, only to hint at the riches of truth in these prophetic songs of the Servant. Jesus who is our model for leadership fulfils them all. Matthew knew at once that he was watching a life he had read about before when he watched the Servant-Lord at work (cf. Matt. 12:15–21), combining sensitivity and strength to bring hope and healing. Further than this we cannot go. Into the fourth servant song in chapter 53 of Isaiah we cannot follow. More than serving, he must suffer. And there is too much in this which is unique to Christ for us to venture far. Except perhaps to say one thing: actions speak louder than words. Redemptively His mission is accomplished but all His servant-leaders in some measure are called to fill up in their flesh "what is still lacking in regard to Christ's afflictions, for the sake of his body, which is the church" (Col. 1:24). We can at least, in our leadership, imitate Paul as he imitates Christ.

The Good Shepherd

Of all the pictures of Jesus given in the Gospels, the one which shows Him as the Shepherd has a particular appeal and special relevance to leadership. It is perhaps difficult for us in an urban and industrial society to realise how widely this concept was once used to depict leadership. Outside the Scriptures, in the ancient world, the shepherd imagery was frequently used to describe secular rulers. In the Old Testament it is a clear and consistent motif. As the history of the flock of God is unfolded so the story of its faithful or unfaithful under-shepherds is recorded. Moses lists the essential functions of such men when he asks God for a new leader to succeed him. "May the Lord, the God of the spirits of all mankind, appoint a man over this community to go out and come in before them, one who will lead them out and bring them in, so that the Lord's people will not be like sheep without a shepherd" (Num. 27:16–17). When the leaders failed in this duty, the prophets revealed the pain and anger in the heart of God, the Lord of the flock. Ezekiel accused the leaders of his day of being false shepherds. In feeding themselves they were guilty of exploiting the sheep. In failing to care for the weak and sick and scattered sheep they were guilty of criminal neglect. In every way they had been domineering in their leadership. It was against such a background that Jeremiah in a Messianic prophecy promised the coming of a true shepherd. (See Ezek. 34 and Jer. 23.) This true shepherd, Isaiah heralded as the one who would rule, feed, gather, carry and lead God's people (Isa. 40:10–11). "I am that shepherd," said Jesus. As the *Good* Shepherd He lays down His life in a unique redemptive sacrifice. As the *Great* Shepherd He rises up in resurrection to confirm the covenant (Heb. 13:20). As the *Chief* Shepherd He returns to reward the faithful undershepherds (1 Pet. 5:4). He is the model for the pastoral ministry, a ministry as much in need of renewal as any of the others. In the tenth chapter of John we have the secrets of a good shepherd.

(i) *The pastor goes through the same door as the sheep.* "The man who enters by the gate is the shepherd of his sheep" (John 10:2). Every leader is first a disciple, every shepherd is also a sheep. True pastors enter into the reality of the Church's life in Christ in the same way as every other sheep. They are not thieves or robbers. Expecting nothing of the people which they do not demand of themselves, such pastors can lead because they have earned the right to do so.

(ii) *The pastor calls sheep by name* (John 10:3), knowing them personally, knowing their names and history, their hopes and dreams. True pastors might well write to the church as Paul did to the Romans and picture each individual in their care (cf. Rom. 16). They know when to carry sheep and when, as it were, to prod them. Every pastor would have more prophetic courage and be unafraid to lose people if he or she realised that not everyone who is on the church roll is their own sheep.

113

(iii) *The pastor brings the sheep out of the fold* (John 10:4). Genuine pastors know that God's flock cannot remain in the cloistered cosiness of the fold but must emerge into the wide world. So the true pastor seeks to break the ghetto mentality of the people, leading them out of their introspection into new adventures for God. This will not always be to their liking. With the rod of spiritual authority and the staff of the Word he may well have to overcome their objections, quell their fears or stir their lethargy by strong teaching and admonition to persuade them to move.

(iv) *The pastor leads from the front.* "When he has brought out all his own, he goes on ahead of them" (John 10:4). The true pastor is not playing a waiting game, taking a cue from the sheep. Nor is the pastor a sheepdog constantly snapping at their heels. True pastors only ask people to do what they are prepared to do themselves. They are willing to stand in front of people, not hide behind them. They may prod them out of apathy or laziness but will never drive the sheep. This is to exercise positive pastoring which does not simply respond to need or react to crises but creates initiatives for God's people to follow.

(v) *The pastor is trusted as a voice.* "The sheep follow him because they know his voice" (John 10:4). Spiritual sheep instinctively know when the voice of the under-shepherd is the voice of God. Strange accents and foreign tones they do not respond to. Once more we see that the authority of a shepherd lies in voicing to the Church the authentic Word of the living God.

(vi) *The pastor guards the entrance to the fold.* There is a sense in which every true pastor can say "I am the gate for the sheep" (John 10:7). Savage wolves, many of them in sheep's clothing, will attempt to enter the fold and must be watched for. Such enemies will not always declare open war but will infiltrate the flock seeking to gain control and dominate others by psychological manipulation. "Keep watch over yourselves and all the flock of God of which the Holy Spirit has made you overseers," is Paul's parting charge to the Ephesian elders. "Be shepherds of the church of God which he bought with his own blood. I know," Paul warns, "that after I leave, savage wolves will come in among you and will not spare the flock" (Acts 20:28–29).

(vii) *The true pastor is not afraid of confrontation*. Unlike the hireling or mere professional, here there is no shrinking from face-to-face encounter with the enemies of the flock. "The hired hand is not the shepherd who owns the sheep. So when he sees the wolf coming, he abandons the sheep and runs away. Then the wolf attacks the flock and scatters it. The man runs away because he is a hired hand and cares nothing for the sheep" (John 10:12–13). The true pastor will always fight for the flock.

(viii) *The pastor feeds the sheep*. Under such careful leadership the sheep "come in and go out, and find pasture" (John 10:9). The concept of feeding and nurturing God's people on a diet of nourishing Bible teaching has now almost vanished. Replaced by discussions groups and childish "fill-in-the-blanks" Bible study sessions, the Church languishes for lack of real food. But the true pastor while eschewing the old ground of well-worn Bible studies, feeds his church with the fresh revelation of the Scriptures and nourishes it with the whole counsel of God. This brings them into abundant life but this life is not an end in itself. Since most of the flocks around Jerusalem in the time of Jesus were destined for sacrifice, the true shepherd will have a clear aim in feeding the sheep. The pastoral ministry will not be tickling ears to please the people or merely keep them happy. It will be fattening them for the offering of themselves as living sacrifices to God (cf. Rom. 12:1f.).

(ix) *He cares for the sheep at personal cost*. "The good shepherd lays down his own life for the sheep" (John 10:11). "Laying down his life for the sheep" is much more modest for the average pastor than it was for Jesus. But it is still costly. It is the laying down of privacy, time and emotional energy. It means being bothered and burdened by the incessant demands of the flock. This can only be done by love. Peter's threefold commission to tend his sheep and feed the lambs was built upon a threefold reaffirmation of his love for the Great Shepherd. This love sets the tone of all pastoral ministry. "Be shepherds of God's flock that is under your care, serving as overseers – not because you must, but because you are willing, as God wants you to be; not greedy for money, but eager to serve; not lording it over those entrusted to you, but being examples to the flock" (1 Pet. 5:2–3).

(x) *The pastor is interested in the whole of God's flock.* "I have other sheep that are not of this sheep pen. I must bring them also. They too will listen to my voice, and there shall be one flock and one shepherd" (John 10:16). Envisaging the coming in of the Gentiles and the restoration of Israel to whom He was at first exclusively sent, the Good Shepherd prophetically declares the ultimate unity of God's flock. We take our cue from Him. Far from being protective or in any way sectarian, true shepherding looks for the re-gathering of all God's people. The true pastor has a sense of history and an eye for prophecy. The true pastor is not out to create a cosy pastoral idyll, sheltered from the realities of life. The aim of pastoral ministry is not to contain but to expand and enlarge the flock. Not content at seeing the pastoral ministry decline into the sheer triviality of routine visiting with polite cups of tea, those today who have the true shepherd's heart will want big things for the flock. "I will bring them together like sheep in a pen, like a flock in its pasture; the place will throng with people. One who breaks open the way will go up before them; they will break through the gate and go out. Their king will pass through before them, the Lord at their head" (Micah 2:12–13)

This was the prophetic spirit of the Great Shepherd who, knowing that the Shepherd was about to be struck down and the sheep scattered, promised to go before them into Galilee after He had been raised from the dead. The "breaker-through" and "breaker-out" is a more dynamic role for a shepherd than we have made room for in our traditional understanding of the pastoral ministry. But since it is His Spirit who is our Chief Shepherd we would do well to follow Him in it.

Notes

1. R.M. M'Cheyne, *Memoirs and Remains* (Edinburgh: The Banner of Truth Trust, reptd. 1966), p.282.

CHAPTER SEVENTEEN

Jesus: His Lessons on Leadership

The training of the Twelve was for Jesus a major priority of His work. To accept His strategy is to accept that training leaders is the first step to evangelising the world. This is the justification for every leadership training programme and indeed for any contribution this book can make. At a time when long-overdue changes are taking place in the Church's patterns of ministry and when there is a widespread unease at our traditional methods of leadership training, the strategy of Jesus is again receiving close attention and study. This is not before time. It is vital in this changing scene to examine closely what He taught His potential leaders and how He trained them.

(i) *He picked the men He personally wanted*. Mark tells us that "he called to him those he wanted" (Mark 3:13). The fact that He did this after prayer only strengthened His confidence in those He selected. For their part as potential leaders, the twelve disciples knew, from the start, that they were part of His heart as well as part of His plans. They were to become His friends not just His pupils. Three of them were to be especially close to Jesus and the nearest anyone came to sharing in His Gethsemane ordeal.

(ii) *He called them to share His life*. "He appointed twelve … that they might be with him" (Mark 3:14). Being with Him was to be the basis of doing things for Him. Jesus lived with His trainee leaders. He gave Himself to them and not merely His principles, spending more time with them than with anybody else. He laid down His life for them in countless ways in the years leading up to the cross, letting them invade His precious privacy by their eagerness to be with Him, letting them try His patience by their slowness in learning from Him. He allowed them to see Him tired, hungry and homeless, schooling them in rejection and preparing them for their future as the "offscourings of the earth" (cf. 1 Cor. 4:11–13). Leadership in His Church, by implication, would be no sinecure.

(iii) *He showed them how to live*. His was true on-the-job training. He demonstrated before He explained. He showed these potential leaders what to do and – what is much harder – how to do it. Seeing Him at prayer with His Father, they ask Him "teach us to pray" with the implication, "like you pray". Having stooped to wash their feet, He reinforces the lesson by saying: "Do you understand what I have done for you? ... You call me 'Teacher' and 'Lord', and rightly so, for that is what I am. Now that I, your Lord and Teacher, have washed your feet, you also should wash one another's feet" (John 13:12–14). As Lord He clearly tells them what to do; as Teacher He equally clearly shows them how to do it.

(iv) *He involved them in ministry*. From distributing bread and baptising converts, His trainee leaders graduated to mission work on their own (cf. Matt. 10:1ff.; Luke 10:1ff.). In releasing them for this He knew that He had to let them make their own mistakes if they were to grow and mature. He was prepared to accept their failures, using the occasion to teach them something more (e.g. Matt. 17:14–21).

(v) *He sent them out in pairs*. "He sent them out two by two" (Mark 6:7). From the start each disciple knew he was not on his own. From the start each trainee leader knew he did not have all the gifts necessary for ministry but needed to be complemented by another. Each apostolic twosome was a microcosm of the Body of Christ and of this Jesus was sowing seeds in their minds. Together they discovered the true interdependence which safeguards all kingdom work.

(vi) *He delegated to them his authority*. "He ... gave them authority over evil spirits" (Mark 6:7). This was a risk for Jesus but He took it for their sake. Any leader is heading for frustration and failure who is given a task to perform but not the authority to carry it out. Jesus never exposes His representatives to that danger.

(vii) *He checked on their progress*. "The apostles gathered round Jesus and reported to him all they had done and taught" (Mark 6:30). He did not leave them in a vacuum but made room for constant feedback on their experience. They questioned Him closely about the reasons for their successes or failures. He answered them, not always directly, but in ways that egged them on to discover more and to ask more searchingly. They learned to face varied reactions to their word and witness and He explained to them how to respond. He was schooling them in the need to be accountable to Him rather than answerable to the world.

The secret of the Lord

But what did Jesus want His potential leaders to know? Without attempting to cover the whole scope of the teaching of Jesus, we focus on two special learning occasions for the disciples. At one key point in His ministry the Lord Jesus called His disciples aside for a time of retreat at Caesarea Philippi. Here He let them into His deepest secrets.

(i) *He taught them to understand His own person*. There was no one they needed to be more sure of than Himself! He drew from them their own estimate of who He was. "Who do you say I am?" (Matt. 16:15). They learned He was the Christ, though He counselled them to keep quiet about it. What He was telling them in the dark, they would, in due course, be able to speak in the daylight; what was being whispered in their ears they would one day soon be free and bold to proclaim from the rooftops. Meanwhile, the secret of the Lord is with them that fear Him. Wherever afterwards their leadership took them, for them there would be no other name given among men worth naming to the world. And three of them would never forget being "eye-witnesses of his majesty" (2 Pet. 1:16).

(ii) *He taught them to live by revelation*. The importance of this has been emphasised in earlier chapters. But here again, in the strategy of Jesus, we see a vital stress on listening to Father for divine revelation. "Blessed are you, Simon son of Jonah, for this was not revealed to you by man, but by my Father in heaven" (Matt. 16:17). The secret is not given secondhand and leaders must hear it and confess it for themselves.

(iii) *He taught them the significance of the Church in His plans*. "I will build my church" (Matt. 16:18). It is to be His building not man's. His leaders would serve Him by serving His Church and by making His aims for it their aims. He sowed seeds in their minds of the Church as a powerful agency of His kingdom, vested with authority. From the outset His intent was clear that "through the church, the manifold wisdom of God should be made known to the rulers and authorities in the heavenly realms" (Eph. 3:10). Protestantism, which has often lacked an adequate doctrine on the Church is now rediscovering the Body of Christ. To be a leader in such a Church was and still is the greatest possible honour.

(iv) *He taught them the centrality of His death and resurrection*. Overcoming their resistance to the idea, when they began to worry about the possibility of His death, He told them it was inevitable. Jesus impressed upon these trainee leaders how necessary was His death in the fulfilling of His mission. "From that time on Jesus began to explain to his disciples that he must go to Jerusalem and suffer many things at the hands of the elders, chief priests and teachers of the law, and that he must be killed and on the third day be raised to life" (Matt. 16:21).

(v) *He taught them the cost of discipleship*. He spelt out to them what becoming a leader in His Church would involve. Unable to carry His unique cross, every potential leader must take up his own and learn to follow on a self-denying road. Never, as their ministry for Him took them across the Ancient World to their appointed martyrdoms or lonely Patmoses, would they ever be able to say He had disguised the cost. But in the light of the price he paid, which of us will argue with David Livingstone when he said, "I never made a sacrifice". Every leader knows from first grade that "a student is not above his teacher, nor a servant above his master" (Matt. 10:24).

If the retreat at Caesarea Philippi was one focal point for seeing what Jesus wanted His potential leaders to know, then the Upper Room was the other. In John's account of the "farewell discourses" as they have been rather prosaically termed, there is an abundance of riches. But I want to pick out just three further points which are significant for understanding how Jesus prepared His disciples for ministry. This ministry, it had now dawned upon them, was to be embarked upon without His physical presence and support.

(vi) *He taught them to trust His words and promises*. "I am telling you now before it happens, so that when it does happen you will believe I am he" (John 13:19; cf. 14:29). He laid His credibility on the line that He meant what He said. Often, "after he was raised from the dead, his disciples recalled what he had said. Then they believed the Scripture and the words that Jesus had spoken" (John 2:22).

(vii) *He taught them to trust His Father.* Here in the Upper Room He merely recapped the long education in faith He had given them. Rebuking their little faith or misplaced faith, He had long been schooling them in the assurance that "Father knows". Sending them out without money or luggage, with nothing but the clothes they stood up in, He had been training them to live by faith and prayer. Now He was sealing this lesson in their hearts. "In that day you will no longer ask me anything. I tell you the truth, my Father will give you whatever you ask in my name ... the Father himself loves you" (John 16:23,27).

(viii) *He taught them to trust the Holy Spirit.* "Do not worry," he had said to them on an earlier occasion, "about how you will defend yourselves or what you will say, for the Holy Spirit will teach you at that time what you should say" (Luke 12:11–12). Now in the shadow of the cross, He reassures them about the advantages to be gained from His going and the Spirit's coming (John 16:7). There is no greater lesson or comfort than this for anyone called to leadership in His Church. The Holy Spirit will lead the leaders into all truth. Apostles will not only recall His mighty works and recount them with wonder but, by faith and through the Spirit, will themselves do even greater works! Prophets will expect the Spirit to disclose to them what is to come. Teachers will rely on the Counsellor to teach them all things and to remind them of everything Jesus said. With relief, evangelists will realise it is not their burden to convict the world of its sin; the Holy Spirit will do this through their word and witness. Unable at one stage to bear the weight of many revelations, they will trust the Holy Spirit to show them what they need to know as and when they need to know it. In short, to His potential leaders, the Lord Jesus promised that charisma, that "Spirit of wisdom and revelation in the knowledge of him", which, as we saw earlier, is our indispensable requirement and His inimitable gift.

Good stewards

Having seen how Jesus trained His leaders and what He wanted them to know, we turn finally to lessons on leadership to be gleaned from other areas of His teaching, especially from the parables. His teaching here will once again not only serve as a measure of our own existing leadership but will set out principles which will help us in the raising up of other leaders.

The concept of "stewardship" was one Jesus frequently employed which has special lessons for leaders in His Church. A "steward" was an estate manager given the task of administering the affairs of his overlord. In a controversial and debatable story, Jesus urged that the affairs of His kingdom should be administered no less shrewdly or adeptly than the affairs of commerce (Luke 16:1–9). Jesus then goes on to show that the point of comparison is not the dishonesty of the steward but his logic. The lesson to be drawn is the inherent connection between our handling of earthly things and our handling of heavenly things. The sons of light need to know this if they are to prepare for the future and exercise leadership in the light of it. The principles of leadership are clearly stated.

(i) The follower of Jesus who is faithful in small things can be expected to handle big things. "Whoever can be trusted with very little can also be trusted with much, and whoever is dishonest with very little will also be dishonest with much" (Luke 16:10). Those who can rule themselves are better fitted to rule others than those who lack self-control. "Like a city whose walls are broken down is a man who lacks self-control" (Prov. 25:28). It is for this reason that a leader in the Church must be "self-controlled ... not given to drunkenness ... not violent ... not quarrelsome" (1 Tim. 3:2–3). On the same basis someone who can manage on the scale of their own household is qualified to be a leader in the larger household of God (1 Tim. 3:4). David could be trusted with his father's flock before he became the shepherd of God's flock. He had won victories over the lion and bear before he tackled Goliath, not in Saul's untried armour but with weapons that he had used successfully on lesser enemies. Faithful in small things, he became ruler of Israel.

(ii) Faithfulness in handling material things qualifies us to be trusted to handle spiritual things. Our attitude to money is a key to our suitability for leadership. For "if you have not been trustworthy in handling worldly wealth, who will trust you with true riches?" (Luke 16:11). This was the test Ananias and Sapphira failed. It was awareness of this principle that made Paul so keen to be self-supporting as far as possible. "I have not coveted anyone's silver or gold or clothing. You yourselves know that these hands of mine have supplied my own needs and the needs of my companions" (Acts 20:33–34). For those leaders who are financially supported by the churches there is the consolation of being in the Lord's will. For "the Lord has commanded that those who preach the gospel should receive their living from the gospel" (1 Cor. 9:14). But the principle applies. "I have learned the secret of being content in any and every situation, whether well fed or hungry, whether living in plenty or in want" (Phil. 4:12). So a leader who is "not pursuing dishonest gain", who is "not greedy for money but eager to serve" is proving faithful in material things, and qualifies to be a leader in the Church (cf. 1 Tim. 3:8; 1 Pet. 5:2).

(iii) People who are faithful in what belongs to someone else can be trusted with their own sphere of responsibility. "And if you have not been trustworthy with someone else's property, who will give you property of your own?" (Luke 16:12). When a Christian applies for secular employment she may well ask the pastor or vicar for a reference to take to a prospective employer. In Christian leadership the reverse procedure might well apply. Before recognising a leader in the Church we might do well to ask his or her employer for a reference to give to us! A prospective leader after all, "must also have a good reputation with outsiders, so that he will not fall into disgrace and into the devil's trap" (1 Tim. 3:7). It is interesting to see how well this principle of Jesus is borne out by scriptural example. Joshua for example, "had been Moses' assistant since youth" before succeeding him as leader of Israel (Num. 11:28). Samuel first served Eli, becoming used to his every beck and call, before he heard the voice of God calling him to be a prophet and judge (1 Sam. 3:5). David, as we mentioned earlier, faithfully served his father Jesse by tending his flock before God entrusted him with leading His people (1 Sam. 17:17–19; cf. Psa. 78:70–72). Elisha was Elijah's valet before eclipsing him as a prophet. He was willing to become Elijah's "attendant" and to be afterwards known as the one who "used to pour water on the hands of Elijah" as his personal servant (1 Kings 19:21; 2 Kings 3:11). Because Timothy proved himself by assisting Paul in his ministry he was entrusted with missions of his own (Phil. 2:22). All these are instances of good stewardship; examples of those who in faithfully discharging their responsibilities to others, qualified to receive ministries of their own.

Each of the three principles we have looked at are facets of a basic law that applies in many areas of truth. It is that "the spiritual did not come first, but the natural, and after that the spiritual" (1 Cor. 15:46). It is the devil, not the Lord that finds work for idle hands to do. The Lord looks for His leaders to working people, calling them like Amos, from their ploughing to be His prophets; taking hard-working if not always successful fishermen and making them into successful fishers of men. This is another way of saying that duty precedes love, that even charity begins at home, that paying your bills may be the first step on the road to preaching the gospel.

One heartening feature of this teaching of Jesus is that it assumes advancement in His kingdom. These principles of promotion in the work of God are sharply summed up in the parables of Jesus, especially the so-called parables of the talents and the pounds.

Both these parables in their context are addressed to leaders, and to leaders who had failed. Both are told against the expectation of the master's absence and eventual return and so contain principles of leadership that apply for all time to Christian leaders "until he comes".[1] From Matthew's account of the story of the talents, we can sum up all we have said about stewardship.

(i) A steward is on *trust*. Calling his servants to him, "he entrusted his property to them" (Matt. 25:14). Leadership implies a trust placed in us. "Now it is required that those who have been given a trust must prove faithful" (1 Cor. 4:2). Paul sees himself as "simply discharging the trust" committed to him (1 Cor. 9:17). It is in the mercy of God that so often for us, as for Paul, He foresees our faithfulness and puts us into His service (cf. 1 Tim. 1:12). To be trusted so deeply gives confidence to any leader. In releasing other leaders, we, too, will look for faithful men and women and trust them to do a work we might well at some stage feel better able to do ourselves.

(ii) A steward is given *ability*. "According to ability" tasks and talents are distributed to each one. Freely we have received, freely we give. The gifts and callings of leadership convey their own sense of ability which gives confidence to Christian leaders that they do not approach people empty-handed.

(iii) A steward is given *responsibility*. Because the master has gone on a journey, the steward is left in charge. The steward has a responsibility to fulfil until the master returns and so accepts leadership not as a sideline or hobby but as a serious duty. "Choose seven men ..." said the apostles. "We will turn this responsibility over to them" (Acts 6:3) This responsibility is often for other servants of the Master (Luke 12:42), to be in charge of them or over them in the Lord (1 Thess. 5:12). A steward acts best if given clear and explicit instructions on what to do. Leaders act best and most responsibly when their roles are clearly defined. Above all leaders need to act upon their responsibility. The gravest indictment laid against stewards is to have failed to utilise what they had been given. "Put this money to work until I come back" is the master's chief concern. It is irresponsible to ignore it. Use it or lose it is a leader's choice. "Whoever does not have, even what he has will be taken from him" (Matt. 25:29).

(iv) A steward is *accountable*. A steward knows by the very terms of engagement that: "From everyone who has been given much, much will be demanded; and from the one who has been entrusted with much, much more will be asked" (Luke 12:48). Every steward lives with the knowledge that the end of the story is: "After a long time the master of those servants returned and settled accounts with them" (Matt. 25:19). Jesus had schooled His trainee leaders in this (cf. Luke 9:10; 10:17ff.) and they were only too ready to be accountable to Him. Accountability gives a sense of security to leaders who know there is someone willing to oversee them and turn even their mistakes to good. It also gives stewards a sense that their work matters and the quality of it is of some concern. Far from inhibiting initiative, accountability positively encourages it. The cautious, do-nothing-for-fear-of-the-consequences attitude is precisely the one attitude that the master finds utterly distasteful in his steward (Matt. 25:24ff.). Leaders who invite followers do so out of the humbling sense of having to "give an account" for each soul in their care (Heb. 13:17)! Presumption in seeking elevated ministry is discouraged by the principle of accountability. "Not many of you," writes James, "should presume to be teachers, my brothers, because you know that we who teach will be judged more strictly" (James 3:1). The reward the steward looks for is not the fruit of self-interest but that promotion which opens further access to the master's joy (cf. Matt. 25:21). This is all part of the fact that to "aspire to leadership is a noble ambition". "And when the Chief Shepherd appears, you will receive the crown of glory that will never fade away" (1 Pet. 5:4).

It was because He knew that good leaders were so vital that the Lord Jesus invested so much in them. As Robert Coleman aptly put it, "If we get the right quality of leadership, the rest will follow; if we do not get it, the rest will have nothing worth following."[2]

Notes

1. More likely, I now see, these parables in original context relate to the current "return of God" to His people Israel, calling in the accounts through His final Prophet, His Son, Jesus, in what was the terminal generation. But their impact remains undiminished.
2. Robert Coleman, *The Masterplan of Evangelism* (New Jersey: Fleming Revell, 1963), p.125.

CHAPTER EIGHTEEN

Jesus: Legacy of Leadership

Jesus, then, had His own way of making leaders. He told them He loved them. He treated them as His friends, taking them into His confidence, opening His heart to them, risking even their rebuke. He teased them with parables, raising in their minds more questions than He was immediately prepared to answer. He taught them how to pray. He told them about His cross, again and again impressing upon them how necessary it was. He taught them the mysteries of His Father's kingdom. He trusted them to do what he could have done better himself. He tested them in experience, schooling them in a "seminary in the streets" rather than sending them to the Qumran Bible College! He interceded for them, not always shielding them from failures but praying them through it so that they emerged stronger and better able to help others. He told them to wait for the Spirit's power before going anywhere. Then, having given them His Spirit, He gave them to the world.

Of all His legacies – His peace, His joy, His meal – none was more significant than the leaders He left to His Church.

"As the Father has sent me, I am sending you" (John 20:21). These words put ex-fishermen and tax-collectors in line with the mission of the Son of God. It is an enormous privilege for any leader to be caught up in the same movement of divine grace that brought the Son of God into the world. Consecration to leadership and ministry takes its rise from the truth of His consecration in the blood of the cross: "As you sent me into the world, I have sent them into the world. For them I sanctify myself, that they too may be truly sanctified" (John 17:18–19). By implication, those He sends are to be as dependent on, and obedient to, the Father as He was. In doing this they will provoke the same reactions as He did. "Remember the words I spoke to you: 'No servant is greater than his master.' If they persecuted me, they will persecute you also. If they obeyed my teaching, they will obey yours also" (John 15:20). Sent as He was sent, His leaders will face the same twofold response He did; some will reject the Word; some will receive it. Truly "apostolic" leadership will always share in this ambiguity and will always have the paradoxes of the incarnation stamped upon it. His servants commend themselves by this ambivalence, "through glory and dishonour, bad report and good report; genuine, yet regarded as imposters; known, yet regarded as unknown; dying, and yet we live on; sorrowful, yet always rejoicing; poor, yet making many rich; having nothing, and yet possessing everything" (2 Cor. 6:8–10).

Elsewhere it is argued (chapter 20) that His gift of the Twelve did not exhaust His gift of apostleship to the Church. This is equally true of all the other ministries needed by the Church. No passage of Scripture is more important in establishing this or more relevant to today's Church, than the fourth chapter of Paul's letter to the Ephesians.

Ephesians 4

The verses which are especially important for our discussion are verses 7–13.

> But to each one of us grace has been given as Christ apportioned it. This is why it says:
>
>> "When he ascended on high,
>> he led captives in his train
>> and gave gifts to men."
>
> (What does "he ascended" mean except that he also descended to the lower, earthly regions? He who descended is the very one who ascended higher than all the heavens, in order to fill the whole universe.) It was he who gave some to be apostles, some to be prophets, some to be evangelists, and some to be pastors and teachers, to prepare God's people for works of service, so that the body of Christ may be built up until we all reach unity in the faith and in the knowledge of the Son of God and become mature, attaining to the whole measure of the fulness of Christ.
>
> (Eph. 4:7–13)

From this passage we learn a number of vital things about the ministries set in the Church.

(i) *They are the gifts of the ascended Christ who is Lord of the Church*
Paul here is quoting and reflecting upon Psalm 68. Having commented
upon the "he ascended" of Psalm 68:18 Paul goes on to comment on
the "he gave" found in the same verse. "He ascended" means that
Christ has returned in triumph to the glory of His Father, so "he gave"
means that in His ascension victory He shares the spoils with His
Church. Because "he gave" is picked up from the quotation from Psalm
68 the past tense does not imply that it happened only once, but that
the ascended Christ is the giver of gifts. This He continues to be. Nor
does the change Paul makes from the "he received gifts" of Psalm 68
to the "he gave gifts" in his version of it alter the picture. For in order
to give gifts you first have to receive them. The obvious parallel here
which has more than verbal significance is the gift of the Holy Spirit.
Of Jesus it was said that "exalted to the right hand of God, he has
received from the Father the promised Holy Spirit and has *poured out*
what you now see and hear" (Acts 2:33). So the Lord Jesus takes cap-
tured rebels and gives them back to His Church as its leaders and ministers. In G.G. Findlay's words, "He gives what he receives. Yet he
gives not *as* he receives. Everything laid in his hands is changed by
their touch." In this way chief prosecutors become chief apostles and
Christ's fiercest opponents become His finest protagonists. Here is the
irony that makes God smile, of "gifts and succour coming to the
Church from unlooked-for quarters and reinforcements from the ranks
of the enemy".[1]

(ii) *These ministries represent the Head of the Church who is Christ*
Apostles, prophets, evangelists, pastors and teachers receive their commission directly from the ascended Lord Himself. Like Paul their pro-
totype, they are not made by men. They do not receive their authority from men. They represent the headship of Christ as the charismata
express His Body. New Testament ministry is a reflex of Christ the
Head of the Church. It derives its permission from the Body of Christ,
but its commission is from the Body's head. Those who stand in this
succession, albeit in lesser measure, are agents of the spiritual authority and rule of Christ in His headship of the Church. As the nervous
system extends the brain to the body so they bring to the Church the

necessary control, vitality, direction and co-ordination it needs to function. In doing so they are called also to show some of the same selfless, sacrificial love and care which the Head shows to His Church (cf. Eph. 5:23ff.).

(iii) *They express together the fullness of Jesus*

No person, man or ministry can adequately represent Jesus. But together the fivefold ministries can bring the Church to an experience of the "fulness of Christ" (Eph. 4:13). Each of the ministries is needed to do this because Jesus was every one of them and each of them is a measure of the gift of Himself (cf. Eph. 4:7). Jesus was the Apostle (Heb. 3:1), the "sent one" of the Father (cf. John 8:42). Jesus was "a prophet, powerful in word and deed" (Luke 24:19; cf. John 4:9; 6:14), in fact, the Prophet, like Moses, who would arise in the last days (Acts 3:22ff.). Jesus was the great evangelist, the preacher of the good news of the kingdom with signs that follow (Mark 1:15ff.; Matt. 4:23ff.).

Jesus was, as we have seen, the Good Shepherd through death, the Great Shepherd through resurrection, the chief of all under-shepherds who pastor His flock (John 10:14; Heb. 13:20; 1 Pet. 5:4). Jesus too was the Teacher who spoke with unprecedented authority and power under the anointing of the Holy Spirit (Matt. 4:23, 7:28–29; Acts 1:1–2). So, "when those with varying ministry gifts are together they will collectively, manifest the singular ministry of Jesus".[2] Through these five ministries Jesus gives Himself again to His Church. We will begin to experience His fullness only when we have them.

(iv) *They complement one another and produce variety*

The apostles, the appointed messengers of Christ to His churches, have a fatherly ministry, laying a foundation of life, obedience and doctrine in each place. The prophets, the seers and spokesmen of Christ to His Church, bring vision to believers, giving them a sense of purpose and direction through the living Word. Evangelists proclaim the good news of the kingdom, heal the sick and cast out demons. Pastors rule and care for the sheep, feeding and fattening them for God. Teachers expound in detail the revelation brought by apostles and prophets, applying the whole counsel of God to the lives of believers and making disciples in the process.

Traditionally, the concept of ministry has been narrowed to that of the pastor–teacher with evangelists forced to work outside the church and apostles and prophets relegated to the limbo-land of yesteryear. But all the ministries are needed in the Church if for no other reason than to produce that essential variety which is a mark of God's handiwork. When a church is monopolised by the ministry of a teacher then the people form an audience and tend to become passive. Often, when the teacher leaves, the listeners leave too. Similarly, where an evangelist works alone without the other ministries, a large number of spiritual babies will be produced with no one to help them grow up and mature. If a prophetic ministry monopolises the body then more often than not the prophet will end up on some mountain top with a tiny handful of elite followers staunchly believing they have received more revelation than anyone else. Unbalanced by any other ministry the pastoral role too, on its own, produces distortion. The sheep become merely fat and woolly, over-cosy and overfed, content to graze and glad to have their ears tickled, but lacking any clear sense of direction. But the ascended Christ gives all five ministry-gifts in order to provide His Church with that richness and variety which can more nearly reflect His own.

(v) *They are ministries for the whole Church*

If, as we shall see, being elders and overseers and deacons are main ministries of the local church, then apostles, prophets, evangelists, pastors and teachers are ministries for the whole Church. Their writ runs throughout the many congregations that make up Christ's Body. They cut clean across denominational allegiances. They break the mould of the independence of the local church. This is what makes their presence, or even the threat of their presence, such a contentious issue today. For it is the restoration of these gifts to the Church that undermines our ecclesiastical structures as nothing else does. Traditions which can absorb or attempt to absorb the baptism and gifts of the Holy Spirit and which can accommodate certain changes in styles of worship, cannot contain such a diversity of ministry and remain the same. The roles of apostles and prophets are, of course, the most disputed. But it is the trans-local nature of these ministries that makes them such a challenge to existing arrangements. Even the "pastor" in Ephesians 4:11 is, I believe, to be seen as a shepherd to the wider Church, rather than as the caring elder of the local church. Timothy was sent to perform this role of the pastor–teacher as an apostolic delegate in many of the churches Paul founded.

(vi) *These ministries bring wholeness to the Church*
The ascended Christ gives the Church such leaders to do four things:

- (a) to "equip" or "prepare" believers for service
- (b) to cause the Church to "be built up" and grow numerically
- (c) to bring believers to maturity both individually and corporately
- (d) to unite the Church.

The Church will be what its ministers are. The Church does not make them. It would be truer to say that such ministries make the Church. Certainly they bring to it a measure of wholeness. No longer are believers childish, spoon-fed and self-willed; they are responsible and caring and supportive of each other. No longer are believers tossed "back and forth by the waves" of mood or emotion, lacking assurance and stability; they are calm and consistent and joyful. No longer are they "blown here and there by every wind of teaching"; instead they are continuing steadfastly in the apostles' doctrine. No longer are believers at the mercy of the "cunning and craftiness of men", the victims of manipulation or church politics; they are enjoying open and honest relationships with their leaders and with one another. No longer are they stuck; they are growing up into Christ in every way. No longer are they fragmented; they are "joined and held together" in a harmony where each knows his place and gift.

Is this picture of wholeness idealistic? If it is then we have grown unduly pessimistic, failing to grasp just what a restoration of all the ministry gifts of the ascended Lord might do for us. Since Christ gives them who are we to refuse them? If we accept these five ministries as given today we need to do three things with them.

(i) *Recognise them*. The Church needs a new boldness in breaking the mould of its own tradition and in beginning to name names and recognise functions. Don't make sainthood posthumous. Call a person a pastor and no one minds. But call them an evangelist and no one quite knows what to do with him. Usually for lack of recognition the evangelist moves off to start a separate mission organisation. Call someone an "apostle" or "prophet" and we are even more discomfited until the results overtake our reticence.

(ii) *Release them*. Antioch was a model church in its ability to see what the Holy Spirit was doing and to respond to His direction. It was willing to see the break-up of its ministry team of prophets and teachers in order to free two of their number for apostolic work. Drastic changes in patterns of ministry and a great release of finances will be required to bring us into the good of the gifts Jesus has for His Church.

(iii) *Receive them*. To receive His servants is to receive Christ Himself. If we receive a preacher because He is a preacher we get a good sermon. But if we receive Him as a prophet we receive a prophet's reward (Matt. 10:40). "Even though my illness was a trial to you," Paul tells the Galatians, "you did not treat me with contempt or scorn. Instead, you welcomed me as if I were an angel of God, as if I were Christ Jesus himself" (Gal. 4:14).

"Function" is a vital word here. Walking round Wisley Gardens, the home of the Royal Horticultural Society, a colleague and I admired a bush with luxuriant foliage and flowers. We tried to identify it but it had grown so much that it had obscured its label! When Jesus gives gifts of ministry to the Church, what they do is in the end more important than what they are called. It is to the varied *functions* of the ministries the ascended Christ gives that we now turn. We do this in the hope that as these fivefold ministries are given room to work in the Church, the growth they produce will obscure their labels!

Notes

1. G.G. Findlay, *Ephesians* The Expositor's Bible (London: Hodder & Stoughton, 1907), p.237.
2. Trevor Martin, *Kingdom Healing* (Basingstoke: Marshalls, 1981), p.117.

Part Four
Leadership Today

CHAPTER NINETEEN

Masterbuilder

"Remember always," wrote Jim Eliot in his journal, "that God has taught you the importance of a *building* ministry."

To bless is one thing; to build quite another. There's no doubt which is harder. To bless people needs charisma and a fast car! It usually results in much appreciation, large love-gifts and return bookings. All of this is good and necessary but it is not enough. Jesus is not blessing the crowds but building His Church. To build with Him is hard work.

A ground plan is first required. The Master Designer is not haphazard. Leaders with desire to build will need insight into the strategy of God for His Church. In close collaboration with those in the team with prophetic insight such leaders will seek to build "according to the pattern" shown to them on the mountain of revelation. Unfortunately, in today's Church we cannot guarantee clear ground to work on. As in Nehemiah's day there is "much rubbish" to remove before building can commence. Some churches have tried to graft the new structure of praise, body-life, cell groups onto the old without changing anything. So the old pattern of meetings, events and organisations competes with the new order of things. The result is chaos and exhausted and confused labourers. Clearing away the accumulated clutter is the only answer. Hand-picking the workers may then be the only way to start. Nehemiah found that not everyone who seemed outwardly keen on joining the reconstruction work was after what he was after (Ezra 4:2–3). There are some people we can well do without if we want to see God's house built. After all, expert builders have been wrong before!

Foundation-laying

To secure the base for building is then the first objective. "According to the grace of God which was given to me," writes Paul, "as a wise master builder I have laid the foundation" (1 Cor. 3:10, NKJV). A New

Testament apostle is an "*architekton*". This means far more than the English word "architect" implies. It conveys the idea of a superintendent of the building process, who oversees its erection. This apostolic function is the necessary basis for every local church which forms part of the household of God "built on the foundation of the apostles and prophets" (Eph. 2:20). What do "apostles" do in laying a foundation?

(i) *They lay a foundation of life in Christ*. "For no-one can lay any foundation other than the one already laid, which is Jesus Christ" (1 Cor. 3:11). Apostolic ministry is a life-source to the Church, walking in the faith footsteps of Abraham a "father of the faithful". To bring people to birth in Christ and to see them established causes much travail and pain until Christ is formed in them (Gal. 4:19).

(ii) *They lay a foundation of obedience to Christ*. The apostolic ministry stresses clearly from the beginning the lordship of Jesus Christ for whom it is pledged to make disciples. It aims to bring about the "obedience of faith" and looks for that obedience to be complete (Rom. 1:5; 2 Cor. 10:6). It strives to help each individual in the Church to build upon the only sure foundation of obedience to the commands of Jesus (Matt. 28:18ff., 7:24ff.)

(iii) *They lay a foundation of doctrine*. Before the Church can go onto maturity the foundational doctrine must have been clearly laid. This is apostolic building work, ensuring that every member of the Church is established on the sure foundation of their death and resurrection with Christ (Col. 2:6ff.). Apostolic ministry contends with every error and distortion that would detract from the fullness of Jesus and would diminish the believer's full experience of Him. Legalism, antinomianism, mysticism, asceticism, pseudo-spirituality – all alike are refuted and corrected, e.g. Galatians, Colossians. For the apostle, the truth is the best basis for building.

Fit for divine habitation

According to the second book of Maccabees, the "master builder is responsible for the whole construction". He supervises the entire work, and is especially concerned for the fitting out of the building for its intended purpose. The brochure I collected from the estate agents when house-hunting stressed the selling points of the property I was interested in: "integral garage, central heating, fitted wardrobes, fully equipped kitchen."

All this suggested it was ready for occupation! Apostolic leadership is similarly concerned for the internal integrity of God's house, that nothing in it is superfluous or unrelated to the stated purpose of the building. Is the central heating of love to be working well so that the building is attractively warm and welcoming? Are the parts of the building fitted and equipped to serve their function? All this is so that the Church may once more be a dwelling place of God in the Spirit (Eph. 2:20–22).

During construction apostolic ministry will measure the house against the plumbline of Jesus (Rev. 1–3) who as cornerstone determines the shape of the building". "Unfit for human habitation" used once to be scrawled on the walls of slums awaiting demolition. "Fit for divine habitation" is now being written once more on the walls of the church undergoing restoration. For this the ministry of apostles under the Holy Spirit is largely responsible.

What is an apostle?

The verb behind the noun "apostle" means "to send forth". It implies that the person sent forth has received a commission to represent the authority which sends him. There is much uncertainty as to how deeply New Testament concepts were influenced by contemporary Jewish practice. The "shaliach" were the legal delegates of the Sanhedrin and although not missionaries did travel with letters of authorisation. Saul of Tarsus was a typical case (Acts 9:2; 26:10). There is a rabbinic saying to the effect that "the one sent by a man is as the man himself". We are on surer ground if we seek a precedent for apostleship in the Lord Jesus Himself. Not only is He the Sent-One of His Father (John 8:42) but He is in turn the Sender of others (Luke 11:49; John 20:21, "As the Father has sent me, I am sending you"). He identifies Himself totally with those He sends so that "He who receives you receives me" (Matt. 10:40).

Apostles are the gift of Christ to His Church. Here we must distinguish carefully between two different kinds of apostles. The distinction that needs to be made is between what might be called "apostles of the Resurrection" and "apostles of the Ascension". The original Twelve, minus Judas, are those who are recommissioned by the Risen Christ. They receive the inbreathing of resurrection life directly from Jesus as the first fruits of His new creation. From Him they receive proof of His being alive and the principles of the kingdom at firsthand. He gives them their orders through the Holy Spirit. Reinforced by Matthias, they receive the promised Holy Spirit at Pentecost. These are the "apostles of the Lamb" with a special place in God's plan (Rev. 21:14; Matt. 19:28). To them Paul must be added as the one who completes the group of "Resurrection apostles". "Last of all, as it were to one untimely born, he appeared also to me" (1 Cor. 15:8, NRSV).

The testimony of this exclusive group forms the basis of the definitive standard of teaching and doctrine for us. We believe Jesus through their word (John 17:20). Strictly speaking, their only true successor is the New Testament itself which preserves the record of their inspired testimony (cf. John 16:12–14). All subsequent apostolic ministry must submit to and accurately reflect this normative apostolic testimony. Their word is primary and is Scripture; any other apostolic word is derivative and scriptural.

Paul, however, is unique and pivotal. For not only is he the last of a series of apostles who have seen the Risen Christ: he is the *first* of a new series of what might be called "Ascension apostles". Not an original member of the Twelve, Paul accepts his call from Jesus without personally referring to them. In describing himself as "untimely born" Paul may well be reflecting this conviction that he was a bridge between the original apostles and their successors. What is clear from Paul's case, is that the apostolic office was not limited to the twelve. The famous Victorian New Testament scholar, J.B. Lightfoot, was surely right in stating that "neither the canonical Scriptures nor the early Christian writings afford sufficient ground for any such limitation of the apostolate".[1] Barnabas, James, the Lord's brother, Julias and Andronicus, Timothy and Silas, are others given an apostolic role. No longer do apostles have to come down from Jerusalem. Antioch is the new starting-point for those commissioned by the ascended Christ through the Holy Spirit. As Paul makes clear to the Ephesians, it is "he who ascended far above all the heavens that he might fill all things" who gives "some to be apostles". Jesus Christ is building His Church still. To that end His ascension gifts of ministry have no more ceased than His ascension gift of the Holy Spirit. Today's Church needs both. What do apostles look like? In writing to the Thessalonians, Paul shows us how apostles can be recognised.

(i) *They like to work as part of a team.* Paul, Silas and Timothy write to the church at Thessalonica. Over 20 men were at one time or another associated with Paul in his apostolic travels. True apostles are not charismatic lone-rangers who lack or even despise the checks and balances of plurality. Rather they relish the tension and joys of peer-level relationships. That is why they can lead others. Keen to move with others, they attract other ministries to them in a complementary team. For the same reason they love to bring on younger people in their calling in God (1 Thess. 1:1). Building together is great wisdom.

(ii) *They demonstrate a measure of spiritual gift and anointing.* "... our gospel came to you not simply with words, but also with power, with the Holy Spirit and with deep conviction" (1 Thess. 1:5). Apostles have spiritual power not ecclesiastical status. Enjoying the charisma of the Holy Spirit they may not be "officially ordained" in today's Church. In this respect those who are beginning to move out in apostolic calling are the first to admit that what they are is embryonic. All those I know covet the "wonders and miracles" which are one of the true signs of an apostle (2 Cor. 12:12). Builders in a spiritual house, they are people of the Spirit.

(iii) *They are verified by their proven character.* "You know how we lived among you for your sake" (1 Thess. 1:5b). These are people of integrity, who have the mastery over wrong motives, and are not out to deceive, flatter or make money from those they minister to (1 Thess. 2:2–6). Such servants of God are worth imitating in order to draw nearer to Jesus (1 Thess. 1:6).

(iv) *They show patience and gentleness.* "As apostles of Christ we could have been a burden to you, but we were gentle among you" (1 Thess. 2:6–7). In faith an apostolic ministry can afford to wait and through love does not need to throw its weight about. Building with living bricks takes time and trouble. Paul describes himself as dealing with the Church "as a father deals with his own children, encouraging, comforting and urging ..." (1 Thess. 2:11). Such fathers to the Church have a concern for "each one" in the family. True apostles are not remote office managers presiding over some new charismatic empire which they lay claim to "covering". True apostles are prepared to spend time with individuals and not just leaders at that. They are "on-site" superintendents of the work.

(v) *They are bearers of the Word of God.* "You received the word of God, which you heard from us" (1 Thess. 2:13). Paul describes himself proudly as "a preacher and an apostle ... a teacher of the Gentiles in faith and truth" (1 Tim. 2:7, NKJV). No one can ultimately be recognised as an apostle who does not have a proven ministry as a preacher or teacher of the Word of God. For it is God's Word which is the root of authority. It is God's indwelling Word which is the source of life and makes a ministry effective (1 Thess. 2:13).

(vi) *They stand or fall by the Church.* "You became imitators of us ... And so you became a model to all the believers in Macedonia and Achaia" (1 Thess. 1:6–7).

(a) Like Peter, apostles should be fellow-elders in a local body. There they can be tested and checked while learning like the rest of us what it means to "submit to one another in the fear of the Lord". As fellow-elders they know the responsibility of rule and pastoral care which leaders in the Church have and as apostles will be able to speak into other churches with greater sensitivity (1 Pet. 5:1f). They will not want the "last word" in a legalistic manner, preferring to find the authority of Christ in agreement with the local eldership.

(b) Because they are sent out by the church to which they belong, apostles carry credentials with them. Those who receive them can expect that they will have worked out at home whatever truth or practice is being commended to them as God's wise counsel (Acts 13:1–3).

(c) And because they are sent out by the church of which they are part, true apostles are eager to return to give their report. "From Attalia they sailed back to Antioch, where they had been committed to the grace of God for the work they had now completed. On arriving there, they gathered the church together and reported all that God had done through them and how he had opened the door of faith to the Gentiles" (Acts 14:26–27). True apostles appreciate being accountable. This gives them a sense of security, saves them from the wrong kind of independence and reminds them that they exist to serve the Body and not themselves. So they want the best for the Church not least because their reputation is at stake! "For what is our hope, our joy, or the crown in which we will glory in the presence of our Lord Jesus Christ when he comes? Is it not you?" (1 Thess. 2:19). They take care how they build so that God's house may be fit for Him to live in.

Apostles today

The more we see what apostles do and are, the more we realise how indispensable their ministry is. The Acts of the Apostles is a book without an ending. It records that what "Jesus began to do and to teach" he continued to do and say through His apostles. The Acts of the Apostles has proved such a consistent source of inspiration to reforming hearts in every generation of the Church because it records the beginning not the end of its story. The teaching of the apostles is as basic as their acts. "They devoted themselves to the apostles' teaching" (Acts 2:42). This teaching needs to be restated in every age as the foundational doctrine of the Church (cf. Heb. 6:1f.). It must be reapplied in every fellowship as the pattern of truth to which each disciple is committed for the shaping of character (Rom. 6:17). Apostolic words and deeds are vital to us. The foundation-laying ministry of apostles is essential if churches undergoing radical change are to come onto clear ground and those wholly new groupings of God's people are to come onto a secure and biblical basis. Apostolic ministry with ability to father the Church, its pastors and people, is a real blessing from God much needed today.

This is, of course, fiercely disputed and long debated. Some, for sincere biblical reasons, rule out the possibility of apostles today. Others scarcely seem able to conceive of any pattern of ministry other than that which history has left us as its confused legacy, concluding that with larger doses of humility and forbearance we shall learn to live with the muddle! One suspects that behind many fine words too much is at stake for anyone to admit we might all have been wrong. There is an alternative. It is not an innovation. It is rightly pointed out that that the Early Church had a flexible approach to its patterns of ministry. But it is precisely in order to take advantage of such flexibility that the new wineskin of apostleship is offered to us as both necessary and desirable.

Is the building finished? Is the Bride ready? Is the Body full-grown or the saints completely equipped? Has the Church attained its ordained unity and maturity? Only if the answer to these questions is "yes" can we dispense with apostolic ministry. But as long as the Church is still growing up into Christ who is its Head, this ministry is needed.

Notes

1. J.B. Lightfoot, *Paul's Letter to the Galatians* (Grand Rapids; Zondervan, reprinted 1962), p.94.

CHAPTER TWENTY

Eye-opener

In Richard Adam's classic story *Watership Down* we share the adventures of a small band of rabbits as they leave their threatened field in search of a new and safer warren. We are introduced to Hazel, the courageous leader, to Bigwig, the brave warrior, to Strawberry, Buckthorn and the rest. And then there is Fiver, perhaps the most interesting character of them all. Fiver is different. More sensitive than the other rabbits, he seems to be on almost constant alert. His body tense, his whiskers trembling, his ears pricked, his eyes staring, his nose sniffing the air, he seems perpetually on watch. It is Fiver who sees what the others don't see, who senses danger and warns others of it. He smells the breath of hope wafted from afar. He exhorts and cajoles his fellow rabbits in order to stir them to action. In short, Fiver is the prophet of the group. He convinces the other rabbits that change is not merely as good as a rest but is necessary for survival. He forces them to make decisions they ordinarily would not want to make. He opens up to them possibilities they cannot at first envisage. Acting on intuition, he frees them from the paralysis of well-tried habit. By following his counsel they are saved.

Prophets have invariably proved to be the "salvation" of the Church. Their importance is not to be measured by the number of times the word "prophets" is used in the New Testament. In fact, only one man, called Agabus, is featured as a prophet in the Acts of the Apostles though others including Paul, are named in this category. But Agabus certainly turned up at a crucial time especially for the Jerusalem church. He appears as a trans-local ministry, fired with the Holy Spirit, with a strongly predictive message from God. Forecasting a severe famine, Agabus stirs up the disciples in Antioch to give money to help the brothers back in Judea (Acts 11:27ff.). Prophecy is as practical as famine relief!

Agabus appears once more in the record of the Early Church in a way which throws further light on the New Testament understanding of prophecy. In apostolic teaching a distinction appears to be made between the gift and the ministry of prophecy. Though all can prophesy by virtue of their baptism in the Holy Spirit, not all are prophets. Though all can "manifest" the gift of prophecy, only some are "appointed" to the ministry of a prophet (cf. 1 Cor. 12:7, 28–29, 14:29ff.). So Agabus arrives at Caesarea to meet Paul who is staying with Philip the evangelist and his four daughters. Although these four girls have the "gift of prophecy", Agabus has the ministry of "a prophet". And it is Agabus, not one of the four girls, who is entrusted with a major directive prophecy for Paul (Acts 21:9ff.).

But in discovering what a prophet is and does we are not restricted to the brief references to Agabus. Evidence of prophetic activity is far more widespread in the New Testament than a concordance might suggest. In fact, wherever the words "revelation" or "mystery" occur we are in touch with prophetic activity (cf. Rev. 1:1–3; 10:7). Much of what the apostle Paul and the apostle John saw comes into this category. The "mystery" which a prophet deals in, is a major New Testament concept. By "mystery" is meant not a hidden truth but a truth inaccessible to man's knowledge which is now revealed by the Holy Spirit. It becomes an "open secret", a manifestation of those plans and dispensations of God which are hidden from human reason and hence must be revealed to those for whom they are intended.[1]

At the heart of this "mystery of the kingdom" is the person of Jesus Christ Himself, in whom the kingdom has come in advance of its final manifestation (cf. Mark 4:11). This is why Jesus is central to the prophet's theme. For both Old Testament and New Testament prophets it is the "testimony of Jesus which is the spirit of prophecy" (Rev. 19:10; cf. 1 Pet. 1:10–11).

The "mystery" has several important dimensions.

- It can be seen as the total purpose of God in redemption made known in the revelation of Jesus Christ (Rom. 16:25–26) who is the embodiment of all wisdom and knowledge (Col. 2:2).

- It can be seen in the indwelling of Christ in Gentile believers (Col. 1:29) and His intimate union with His Church (Eph. 5:29), which ultimately includes Jewish and Gentile believers in one body as one New Man (Eph. 3:3–6).

- It can be seen in the present rejection of Israel being to the benefit of the Gentiles in such a way that must still lead to the recovery of Israel to faith in her Messiah (Rom. 11:25–26).

- It can be seen in its final form in the restoration of all things and their summing up in the lordship of Jesus Christ (Eph. 1:9–10) which will involve believers in putting on resurrection bodies like Jesus' own (1 Cor. 15:50–51).

All this is the burden of the prophet who is concerned to open our eyes to these dimensions of the "mystery" and to spell out their implications for us. Prophets will therefore always want us to see four things.

(i) Prophets will want to show us *what God is up to in history*. They will open our eyes to the overall plan of salvation. They will not allow us to become locked in to any one culture or epoch. They will insist that God's strategy is bigger than any exclusive national expression and more far-reaching than any temporary phase. To use an old cliché, the prophet stops the Church marrying the spirit of the age, knowing she will be widowed in the next. The prophet strives to prevent the Church becoming bogged down in details or preoccupied with non-essentials. Prophets force us to stand back and take the larger view. When they sense we have lost our way they seek to get us back on course; if we become stuck they urge us to move again. Like their biblical predecessors, contemporary prophets vividly interpret redemptive history. In this way they give our puny efforts significance by relating them to the total purpose and victory of God in Christ.

(ii) The prophets will want to show us *what the Church is really meant to be*. They are concerned for the shape of the Church, for the form it takes in the world. The prophetic yardstick for the Church is Jesus and it is an act of pastoral care ruthlessly to apply it (cf. Rev. 1:1–3). Anything in the Church which obscures Jesus from a needy world, comes under such scrutiny. Inevitably, prophets challenge accepted ideas and hallowed habits with a view to making Jesus more visible in His Body. They aim to uproot unrighteousness from the Church and to bring judgement to the household of God. They give the Church purpose, set goals to be achieved, bring much needed order to the Body of Christ and give it clear direction. The Church, insists the prophetic voice, exists for God and the world, not for itself. Its worship, its fellowship life, its shepherding should all have a clear prophetic root. Prophetic ministry strives to break any ghetto mentality and to implement God's intent "that now, through the church, the manifold wisdom of God should be made known to the rulers and authorities in the heavenly realms" (Eph. 3:10). Always the prophet keeps before the eyes of the Church the vision of the One New Man.

Prophecy involves dramatic action intended to motivate God's people to be doers of the Word and not hearers only. The symbolic actions of the Old Testament prophets were the isolated and sometimes eccentric acts of individuals. Today the prophet is passionate to ensure that the whole Church has a prophetic lifestyle – a lifestyle of simplicity, of sacrificial love and truthful speech which will give credibility to its message. The prophet works to produce sacramental men and women who once truly immersed in the dying and rising of Jesus will become broken bread and poured-out wine for one another and for the world. Through anointed prophets the Church will become, like her Lord, "mighty in word and deed".

(iii) The prophets will want to show us *what is going on in the world*. They will be aware of world events though not preoccupied with them and will keep reminding the Church that it does not merely exist to preserve certain timeless truths. Rather, prophets will show the Church that it is part of a historical movement, with roots in history and by its own faith and response able to shape history. The prophetic ministry will eschew date-fixing, not pretending to know better than Jesus the day or the hour. But prophets will have a keen sense of the seasons in God's dealings with His people. Aware of the undercurrents of evil in the world not just of its more blatant manifestations, prophets save the Church from moralistic reactions and enable it in turn to be truly prophetic in its judgements. Like a true son of Issachar a prophet understands the times and knows what God's people should do. Quick to detect movements of God's Spirit, the prophet stirs the Church to respond.

(iv) The prophet, finally, will want to show *what is coming from the future*. I put it this way so as to avoid the impression that a prophet predicts the future in a detached or analytical way. Rather the prophet presents a future open to the grace of God, and in this prospect there is nothing rigid or deterministic. The fixed points are promises of personal appearances and personal resurrection. The certain fact of judgement to come makes moral decisions crucial now. The prophet brings the future into today and exhorts the Church to live in the light of it. True hope thus replaces wishful thinking.

Prophets are the enemy of fatalism and the friend of faith. They oppose panic but resist passivity just as strongly. Their view of the future is attractive enough to drive the Church to its knees in prayer and sure enough to keep it on its toes in eager anticipation. For the prophet the "End" is not so much a distant date in a diary as the "final state of affairs". In this sense it is always at hand, pressing in on the Church to shape its thinking and action. By the Spirit the prophetic voices show us the things that are to come as and when we need to know them. They detect the cloud no bigger than a hand which will break with blessing on our heads. They show us what the future can become, that it is not all fixed and settled but awaits our response and engagement. So prophets argue for flexibility in the Church, with nothing permanent that isn't scriptural, with everything possible that is initiated by the Spirit.

In this way, the Church is enabled to glimpse things which eye cannot see in any other way than by the prophet. Seeing this, the Church is challenged to change and to do nothing that is incompatible with the glorious end now staring it in the face. So the prophet will prove an uncomfortable gift. Prophets will object when things seem to be running too smoothly or along well-established lines. When everything is weighed up in advance, when predictability threatens to stifle faith, the prophets will be moved to protest and to plead with the Church to make room for the surprises of the Holy Spirit.

Doors of perception

Unlike their biblical predecessors, the prophets today, of course, are not the original source of definitive and normative doctrine. Then, prophets were part of the unique and inspired revelation of Scripture. Now they are part of the necessary but secondary process of unveiling this previous revelation to the current generation. This needs to be said to guard against any misunderstanding of the position I am adopting. Sadly, the "faith once delivered to the saints" has often been distorted or totally obscured by extra-biblical revelation purporting to come from God through a self-appointed visionary or prophet. To acknowledge this is not to go back on our conviction that the prophet is a valid ministry today but merely to emphasise the proper limits under which it operates. Only that prophetic ministry is valid which ratifies, clarifies or confirms the written Word of God, the Bible. Having said that, we are now in a position to show that the ways in which today's prophet opens our eyes are similar to the ways employed by the biblical counterparts.

What do prophets characteristically do?

(i) *They describe what they see*. Originally, the prophet was a "seer", the "eye" of the people of God (Isa. 29:10). Amos tells us what "he saw concerning Israel". Much of the New Testament revelation is an unfolding of visionary experience undergone by the apostles. Peter saw the "catholic" Christ unfettered by Judaistic inhibitions; Paul saw the "crucified" Christ now glorified and identified with his suffering body; John saw the "cosmic" Christ, the *"Pantokrater"* to whom all the kingdoms of this world submit. So today the prophetic ministry brings God's point of view to the Church. From prophets we learn that God's views are good news. Prophets envision the Church and their oversight seeks to ensure that God's plans are carried out. Prophetic insight penetrates to the real issues that have to be resolved; prophetic foresight anticipates the changes that have to be made. Though subordinate to the authoritative Word of Scripture, the prophet nevertheless throws light on God's will and ways with the force and vividness of an eye-witness. The message is secondary but not secondhand because its source is the living God. Prophets not drugs unlock the "doors of perception".

(ii) *They speak what they hear*. Prophets are the listening ear of the

Church, privy to the divine secrets, sharing in the divine council (Jer. 23:18). Isaiah eavesdrops on heaven's cabinet meeting. Abraham and Moses are prophets because they are the friends and confidants of God. Like them, the prophet today is pre-eminently God's mouthpiece. Who can doubt that this ministry is needed or is often sadly lacking.

Many contemporary debates about the Church and its interface with the culture appear to be carried on with little or no substantial theological argument. This is tantamount to admitting that God does not get a word in edgeways, that His point of view is seldom represented. This is all too common in some sections of the Church where its so-called "prophets", as we noted in an earlier chapter, are merely echoing what is being said by sociologists and other trend-watchers. Our hectic, over-stimulated and over-stimulating society is a poor breeding ground for those whose primary need is silence, meditation and listening. Sometimes for this reason prophets retreat into solitariness in order to hear God clearly once again, and to regain a sense of priorities. It is not tragedy but triviality which wears out the prophetic soul.

(iii) *They show what they feel.* Having touched on this in an earlier chapter, it is enough to emphasise briefly that prophets represent the heart of God as well as His voice. Sometimes the emotions of God will conflict with the prophets' own natural feelings. Jeremiah's patriotism in face of national danger and Ezekiel's mourning in bereavement were both over-ridden in order to communicate God's own feelings to His people. The prophet is not a spiritual fax-machine but embodies the message, expressing the anger and anguish, the joy and compassion of the sending God. Yet for the same reason their own lifestyle can confirm or contradict the message they bring. By their fruits of conduct and faith they are known.

(iv) *They ask questions.* "The prophets," as Heschel says, "do not offer reflections about ideas in general. Their words are onslaughts, scuttling illusions of false security, challenging evasions, calling faith to account, questioning prudence and impartiality."[2] Prophets will ask awkward questions to uncover the truth. "Is it a time for you yourselves to be living in your panelled houses, while this house remains a ruin?" (Hag.

1:3). "Will a man rob God?" asks Malachi as he finds the people with-holding their tithes.

The Old Testament prophets "searched intently and with the greatest care, trying to find out the time and circumstances to which the Spirit of Christ in them was pointing" (1 Pet. 1:10). There is a certain God-centred prophetic restlessness, a participation in the divine discontent with the way things are. The role of prophetic ministry, filled with the same Spirit of Christ, will be the spiritual equivalent of keen investigative journalism. It will inquire into the credibility gap between what we profess and what we are. It will expose the discrepancy between the ideal and the actual. It will ask whether opportunities have been deliberately ignored through cowardice or compromise on the part of the Church. It will probe possibilities for advance and progress that lethargy had overlooked. Its searching questions prod the Church awake and keep the Church alive. Any community that responds self-protectively to such questioning by justifying or defending itself unthinkingly is fast on the way to becoming an institution. When the prophet is fended off in this way, then, "the adventure is over".[3] I use the word "unthinkingly" because it is the role of the prophetic ministry to force the Church to think about what it is doing and why it is doing it.

(v) *They bring the "now" word from God.* Truth which is too generalised is ineffective. Even the Word of God can be so systematised into concepts and doctrines as to lose its impact and thrust. If this happens then we have lost the sense of a Living Voice addressing us, confronting and consoling us. Ensnared in a routine of cyclic Bible studies, we almost imperceptibly lose the ability to know when God is actually speaking to us. In my own experience I found that a precondition of any renewal was to restore to the people the sense that God might actually be speaking specifically to them about certain definite things. It is this which the prophetic ministry brings home to the Church. His message, in Tozer's words, "must alarm, arouse, challenge; it must be God's *present* voice to a *particular* people".[4] So the prophet personalises and contemporises the timeless Word of God, even challenging complacent assumptions based on previous revelation. So Amos warns that the Day of the Lord for which the people long may not turn out to be quite what they expect (Amos 5:18). Once God may have said

"Peace, peace" but He is not saying it *now* and to believe that He is when there is no peace is to be lulled into a dangerously false sense of security. The prophet will not allow us to lock God's Word up in the past, so that what God has once said makes us immune from what He is now saying. Entrusted with the "now" word of God the prophet may appear one-sided. This is one reason for the plurality of ministry described earlier. But even so to try to balance up the prophetic message too soon will blur its impact. Before we react by saying "But, on the other hand", we need to hear God's voice clearly. Harry Blamires has pertinently compared the scholar with the prophet (or thinker). The scholar, he says, "evades decisiveness; he hesitates to praise or condemn; he balances conclusion against conclusion so as to cancel out conclusiveness; he is tentative, sceptical, uncommitted". But the prophet "hates indecision and confusion; he is dogmatic and com-mitted; he works towards decisive action".[5] Jacques Ellul has neatly summarised the dialogue between a prophet and his hearer.

> Yes or no, this time, will you listen to this Word of God?
> But I already heard it yesterday.
> We are now living today.
> It's all the same.
> But you are not the same, you have to decide today.[6]

(vi) *They evaluate the past* by interpreting to God's people "the ways of God in history". It was prophets who wrote the history of Israel endeavouring to bring out the underlying purpose and outcome of God's dealing with His people (cf. 2 Chron. 9:29). Prophets trace for us the real movements of God and highlight their true lessons, by dis-tinguishing them from all human traditions. Seemingly minor events are shown to have major significance. Writing Israel's history the prophets pass over whole tracts of time, summarising a king's reign in a sentence as good or evil, measuring everyone small or great, against the yardstick of God's will. Today, prophetic ministry has the respon-sibility of being conversant with Church history. It will help us to see why the Church is the way it is and the world is the way it is. Knowing the Church's record of revival and declension, the prophetic applies the true lessons of the past to rouse God's people to be "the genera-tion that seeks God's face".

(vii) *They lead the way forward.* There is much to suggest that in its earliest days prophets directed the Church's life under the inspiration of the Holy Spirit. In Luke's account of the Early Church "prophets play a large part and determine the Church's most important decisions".[7] As the analogy of Antioch implies, prophets take precedence in a local church in the direction of its affairs, especially its strategy and forward planning. Prophetic leaders point the way forward and then keep the church moving on its true course. Hosea reflects on the role of Moses as leader of Israel: "The Lord used a prophet to bring Israel up from Egypt, by a prophet he cared for him" (12:13). In leading the Church forward, the prophets may often have to break down what obscures the view. Laying an axe to the root of even (perhaps especially) sacred trees, they act as true radicals. But they tear down only with a view to building again on clear ground. A true prophet is stirred with faith and therefore will never be a destructive critic or disillusioned cynic. There are plenty of people who can tell you what is wrong with the Church – it's not too difficult to do so! Such people are not necessarily prophetic. A leader with a prophetic ministry will not snipe from the sidelines, but will be one with the people, leading them into new experiences of the living God. This, incidentally, is why prophets today, as they once did, should lead us in worship and praise.

(viii) *They are motivators.* The prophet opens the eyes of God's people to strengths and achievements they scarcely feel capable of. The prophet is an exhorter, unwilling merely to show the vision and leave people to it. When Zerubbabel and Joshua began to rebuild Jerusalem, we read that "the prophets of God were with them, helping them" (Ezra 5:2). Later it is recorded that "the elders of the Jews continued to build and prosper under the preaching [or prophesying] of Haggai the prophet and Zechariah, a descendant of Iddo" (Ezra 6:14). It is said of Judas and Silas, themselves prophets, that they "said much to encourage and strengthen the brothers" (Acts 15:32). One senior pastor under whom I once worked, Mike Pusey, exemplified his "patron saint", Barnabas, who earned his nickname because he was a son of *"paraklesis"* or encouragement. When we recall that such prophetic encouragement was crucial to Paul in the amazing aftermath of his conversion and was instrumental in launching him into his own ministry, we will not underestimate this aspect of the prophet's word. In Robert

Brow's fine words, "It is not just a question of a little word of building up and a few consoling thoughts. The building up is lifting men and women out of the humdrum into the great movement of God in history. The encouragement of real "*paraklesist*" is the application of the Holy Spirit, the Paraclete himself, to shake man to the very core and stand him on his feet again to do exploits for God."[8]

These, then, are the various ways in which, to its own measure, today's prophetic leadership can emulate its biblical predecessors. As contemporary apostles lay a foundation, in every place of life, doctrine and obedience, so today's prophet lays a foundation of revelation, vision and direction. As a result of its perpetual introspection the Church is not short of opinions and answers. But as DeVern Fromke points out "answers will never work where unveilings are needed".

The prophetic ministry is needed at every level of the Church's life to preserve its integrity and freedom. Without the prophet the Church becomes a "spiritless organisation" in which even apostolic work hardens into a new form of religious bureaucracy. Without the prophetic thrust, the teaching ministry perpetuates a cycle of timeless truth but is deaf to what the Spirit is now saying to the churches. Similarly, as Jim Wallis notes, "Without a prophetic voice challenging God's people to lay down their lives in the world, pastoral nurture can easily degenerate into self-serving group welfare or inward and unbiblical withdrawal."[9] Evangelism, too, desperately needs to hear the prophet if its methods are to be as godly as its message, and if it is to avoid giving stereotyped answers to questions which people are not asking.

"I am sending you prophets" is a heartening promise from the Lord Jesus to today's Church. *For too long conventional ministerial training colleges have been non-prophet making organisations.* But thankfully, and not before time, the Spirit is raising up a new breed of prophetic people. In my view prophets are a risk the Church must take.

Notes

1. W. Bauer, translated and edited by W.F. Arndt and F.W. Gingrich, *A Greek–English Lexicon of the New Testament and Other Early Christian Literature* (Chicago/Cambridge: University of Chicago Press/Cambridge University Press, 1957), p.532.
2. A. Heschel, *The Prophets* vol.2, p.xv.
3. Paul Tournier, *The Adventure of Living* (London: SCM Press, 1966), pp.36–37.
4. A.W. Tozer, *Of God and Men* (Harrisburg: Christian Publications, 1960). p.24.
5. Harry Blamires, *The Christian Mind* (London: SPCK, 1963), pp.50–51.
6. Jacques Ellul, *The Politics of God and the Politics of Man* (Grand Rapids: Eerdmans, 1972), pp.50–51.
7. Edward Schweizer, *Church Order in the New Testament* (London: SCM Press, 1961), p.72.
8. Robert Brow, *Twenty Century Church* (Eastbourne: Victory Press, 1968), p.57.
9. Jim Wallis, *The Call to Conversion* (Oxford: Lion, 1981), pp.128–129.

CHAPTER TWENTY-ONE

Instructor

In the Scriptures a variety of fascinating metaphors are used to describe "the Word of God". In particular it is interesting to note that the "Word" is likened not only to "a seed" but also to the "water" that nourishes the seed and causes it to grow. "Let my teaching fall like rain," Moses prays in expectation (Deut. 32:2; cf. Isa. 55:10–11; 1 Cor. 3:6). The Word of God has to be sown deeply in our lives. Once this is done, an ongoing ministry of the Word is needed to water the seed of life and bring it thrusting through the ground. The teacher's aim is to nourish the life of God implanted in others until it blossoms into confident openness before God and the world, able to bear whatever fruit God intends it to produce. In short, it is clear that in the New Testament the specific aim of the ministry of the Word is to bring believers to maturity. Paul stresses this in writing to the Colossians. "We proclaim him, admonishing and teaching everyone with all wisdom, so that we may present everyone perfect in Christ" (Col. 1:28).

Before we look at this we need to note three things.

(i) The ministry of the Word is a "stewardship" from God (Col. 1:25). God entrusts us with the message of salvation, with the very Word of life, with the awesome task of interpreting the Scriptures for our day. We are to be workmen who do not need to be ashamed, "handling accurately the word of truth".

(ii) The steward's objective is "to present … the word of God in its fulness" (Col. 1:25). The strong and exciting implication here is that by ministering the Word we are actually fulfilling God's purpose in the world. Because the gospel is no gospel until it is received as good news and takes root in human lives, the actual preaching of it is part of the saving plan. When we speak God's Word we are not merely describing or even explaining something that has happened or is about to happen. Speaking God's Word is a truly prophetic activity in that it helps to bring into being what is being spoken of. We extend and prolong the gospel by the very act of declaring it.

(iii) The subject of the steward's ministry is the "mystery that has been kept hidden for ages and generations, but is now disclosed to the saints" (Col. 1:26). It is a joy to be allowed to share open secrets (cf. Matt. 10:26–27). Even though others cannot grasp the meaning of our word without the intervention of the Holy Spirit we are still obligated to present clear and unambiguous revelation to them. Christian ministry is not a special branch of the secret service. A relative of mine once heard a sermon on "the beast" in the Apocalypse in which twenty-seven different interpretations of its identity were given. Now "the beast" is in the Book and you may have to deal with it. But to leave your hearers with twenty-seven different ideas buzzing around in their heads is not teaching towards maturity! We are dealing with "mysteries" but not with mystification! We live in an era in which God's purposes are manifest to us in a way that they were not even to the great heroes of faith of Hebrews chapter 11. By grace we are "in the know" and it is an exciting privilege to be called to communicate what we have been shown as faithful witnesses.

With these provisional points in mind, we turn to the various forms this communication takes.

Proclaiming Christ

Because the medium is part of the message when it comes to imparting spiritual truth, we need to watch that our methods are as godly as our message. This is why *proclamation* holds such a key place in God's economy. It is no accident that God committed Himself to saving the world through the preaching of the cross. He has not done this because preaching was the only method available to him in an unsophisticated pre-media age. He chose this way quite deliberately. He has ordained that spiritual truth is ultimately transmitted by one person who, standing in the flesh in front of other human persons, communicates to them through human personality and anointing the very word of life. This is simply a consequence of the incarnational principle which makes our gospel so distinctive in the world. To doubt the value of what is called "propositional truth" – the view that truth can be put into words – is really to deny Jesus Himself. For this was precisely what He did. As the unique embodiment of the Word of God, He stood on the earth and spoke eternal truth to those who listened to Him even if they did not always understand Him. "What we have heard" as well as seen, recalls the aged apostle John, still wondering at the fact, constitutes the revelation of that Word of Life which was from the beginning.

So, Paul tells the Colossians, "*we proclaim* Christ" (Col. 1:28). Not everyone who reads this will be in a position to be a proclaimer of the Word. Some may aspire to be. There is no greater privilege for me than to be called to proclamation. "*Katangello*" is the Greek word for it. It certainly does not mean to have a chat or give a little homily. To proclaim means "to have the intention of celebrating, of publicly commending and openly praising". This is what we do when we proclaim Christ. We celebrate him, openly and publicly, commending him with praise as Lord and Saviour and Messiah. This is the foundation of bringing believers to maturity.

"Preaching Jesus" is not the simplistic exercise some have made it. It is not merely an invitation to "come to Jesus". The kind of Jesus Paul is proclaiming he describes to the Colossians. The Christ is the first-born of all creation, the image of the invisible God, who has reconciled all things by his blood and is now, as the first born to rise from the dead, the head of the Church, preeminent in everything. In order to bring others to maturity we need to present believers with the overall purpose of God and show them Christ's central place in it.

Those who minister God's Word must teach this big view. They should teach the details as well, of course, for they are vital. But they should start with the big view. Newer Christians often ask: "We have all the pieces, we have been taught forgiveness and the Spirit and authority and body-life and much more beside. What we want to know is how it all fits together." A comprehensive view of God's strategy needs to be presented which shows how everything holds together in Christ. Understanding tactics is important but grasping strategy is the first priority. When I was a small boy my father often lifted me onto his shoulders at football matches so that I could have a good view of the whole match. As ministers of the Word we have to do just this for those learning from us. Of course, we do need to get down to wash their feet, but equally we must lift them up and sit them on our shoulders, so to speak, giving them a vantage point from which they can survey the whole drama of redemption.

The "now" word is important in ministering the Word. But we do well not to neglect "the whole counsel of God" which sets the "now" word in its proper context and in so doing helps to make it true. Watch someone tackling a jigsaw puzzle. They start by tipping all the pieces into an awful heap in the middle of the table. Then slowly they begin to arrange an outer framework of edge pieces. All the time, while building the jigsaw, they are careful to do one other thing: and that is to keep referring to the picture on the box. So it is with us as we handle lives that are still being put together. Having given them an initial framework of truth, we need continuously to show them the picture on the box by proclaiming Christ to them as the One to whom all things are heading as their final conclusion. Instructed in how to talk and walk and fellowship with this Christ, growing believers will find Him more than adequate to deal with all their needs and will start to become part of the answer rather than part of the problem.

Admonishing

Admonition is another form the Word takes in bringing people to maturity. It operates on a smaller scale than proclamation and has to do with instruction at a personal and intimate level. To "admonish" translates the Greek word "*noutheto*" which means "to set in the mind". In our context it means to set truth in the minds of disciples with a view to changing their behaviour and attitudes in a way that will make them more mature.

Unfortunately, admonition has acquired a very aggressive connotation. This ought not to be the case. For to set truth in someone else's mind is with a view to liberating them not dominating them. It is a truly prophetic function; one fulfilled by the prophets of the Old Testament who are said to have admonished Israel (Neh. 9:30). Nathan did this to David when he confronted the king over his sin against Uriah. In the parable of the ewe-lamb, Nathan set truth firmly in David's mind. "You are the man, David." This is admonition. It involves honest person-to-person mentoring, and sometimes, confrontation. Jesus did this quite naturally by talking with His disciples, being open with them, by turns encouraging, commending and correcting them, but all the time setting truth in their minds. We will never help people achieve maturity by sending memos to them. There has to be a consistent face-to-face admonition.

The subject of admonition is the same as the theme of proclamation. As proclamation presents the vision of Christ, so admonition seeks to set Christ clearly in the minds of those being instructed. In this way the preaching of the glory of Christ is broken down and applied practically to the believer's character and attitudes. Paul did this with the Philippians. He did not set out to deliver a major discourse on the pre-existence, humiliation and glory of Christ. He was initially dealing with a pastoral problem in Philippi of squabbling between certain members of the church there. What these believers need is to "have the mind of Christ". Though one with God Christ "did not consider equality with God something to be grasped made himself nothing ..." (Phil. 2:6ff.). "Your attitude should be the same as that of Christ Jesus" is Paul's way of admonishing them. This is a consistent apostolic method. Is there trouble between Jewish and Gentile members of the Church? Then, they are admonished to "welcome one another as Christ welcomed you". When Paul wants a response to his famine relief appeal, his approach is the same. "For you know the grace of our Lord Jesus Christ, that though he was rich, yet for your sakes he became poor, so that you through his poverty might become rich" (2 Cor. 8:9). Numerous other instances could be quoted (e.g. Eph. 5:1,25; Col. 3:13). What is happening here is that the Christ who is being proclaimed is also being set in the minds of disciples in order to produce mature and Christ-like attitudes and actions.

There are important prerequisites to doing this.

(i) We must have a bridge of relationship with someone before we can admonish him. Too often Christians have fired words and hurled advice at one another as if admonition were a re-make of *High Noon*.

True exhortation involves "*paraklesis*", a drawing alongside of others in a spirit of love and humility. A disciple is not a client, not even a counsellee, but a friend.

(ii) This implies that admonition is best given in the normal flow of life as men walk along together. Words of knowledge, wisdom, correction and encouragement can be shared quite naturally as we enjoy each other's company. Admonition does not have to be stored up for a fateful appointment in the diary. There is a certain type of person with "something on their mind" who books to see you only when they have a complaint to make. Their very outline through the front door glass is enough to make you groan. But true friends have reached my heart when in the course of conversation, often while travelling together, one has said to me "And by the way, Phil ..." "That's right" has been my reply; "That's good ... you really feel that? ... Thanks for pointing that out ... I really hear you on that."

(iii) So admonition calls for a basis of understanding between us. It falls on deaf ears if given to what the Proverbs call a "scoffer", someone too rebellious or too flippant to take anything seriously. But like "an ornament of fine gold is a wise man's rebuke to a listening ear" (Prov. 25:12). Paul and Peter had a sufficiently deep understanding between them for Paul to rebuke his fellow apostle for inconsistency without losing his respect or friendship. "I opposed him to his face," Paul writes, "because he was clearly in the wrong" (Gal. 2:11). Even in apostolic circles admonition has a part to play in bringing men on to greater maturity. It is a healthy sign when leaders give each other the right to intervene in this way in one another's lives. And the face-to-face aspect cannot be minimised or avoided. Some things are too important to be left to hints or inference. To want to manipulate change is very tempting but to walk in openness, speaking the truth in love, makes for maturity among all concerned.

(iv) We must never admonish unfeelingly or ungraciously. We cannot set Christ in someone else's mind if He is not first in ours. It is self-defeating to attempt to encourage Christlikeness by doing it in an un-Christlike way. As we have had cause to note before, Paul admonished the Ephesians with many tears (Acts 20:31). Efficiency is returning to the Church and this is good. But the Church is not a business, nor can its affairs be conducted as if it were. As leaders in the Body of Christ we are not marketing products but making people. Pastors soon find out that people are a lot less tractable than products, less cut and dried than principles. It is infinitely harder to change people than it appears on paper. For our admonition to be effective we will need to "Rejoice with those who rejoice; mourn with those who mourn" (Rom. 12:15). Leaders cannot afford to apply even biblical principles coldly or legalistically.

(v) A prerequisite for admonition is goodness. "I myself am convinced, my brothers, that you yourselves are full of goodness, complete in knowledge and competent to instruct one another" (Rom. 15:14). Before we can admonish others they need to be sure that we are out to do them good not put them down. Some people have approached me with advice which I might have needed but, suspecting that their intentions were to disqualify me rather than edify me, I disdained their counsel. At the same time I have accepted admonition from others because I knew they were concerned for my best interests. This is at once a fatherly and brotherly ministry (1 Cor. 4:14; 2 Thess. 3:15) and both terms pick up the atmosphere in which it best takes place. At this point pastors need to be prophetic and prophets pastoral. Pastors whose sensitivity makes them loath to confront and prone to fudge the issue need the prophetic determination to set truth in people's minds in order to free them. Prophets eager to burst in with a "thou art the man" rebuke, will check themselves and seek the tact and discrimination of the Holy Spirit. And because admonition is born of the goodness in a leader's heart, it will be served up with lashings of genuine encouragement and appreciation.

Before we leave the subject of admonition, there are several dangers attending it which needs to be mentioned.

(i) Don't allow those you admonish to become wholly dependent on you. Failure here breeds a new kind of priestcraft in which disciples become parasitic on the counsellor. Some counselling manuals open the way for this error by fostering the image of a professional consultant dispensing pastoral advice through acquired techniques. But our aim is maturity in others. And to be mature is to be so trained in righteousness as to be able to make accurate moral judgements of one's own (cf. Heb. 5:14). One safeguard is to remember that though a pastor may be in the best position to give such counsel, true admonition is the responsibility of *all* the members of the Body (Col. 3:16). No one has a monopoly of wisdom and, as James Denney once commented, "admonition is better than gossip".

(ii) Don't admonish lightly or carelessly. Another danger is that admonition is offered without the framework of respect and humility it needs to bring godly results. Like the man who approached Jesus to ask for adjudication in a disputed matter, some people simply want their own decisions rubber-stamped by an authority figure. Others "shop around" for the advice which fits their pre-determined plans. So admonition, as with all counsel, should not be offered indiscriminately.

(iii) Don't be domineering when admonishing. Admonition should never be coercive. "I'll do it not because I think it's right but because you say so" is the kind of response which wise leaders will reject immediately. The mind, not the will, is the immediate target of biblical admonition. Understanding what the will of God is must be the primary incentive to change. Otherwise what is produced is a mere slavish adherence to "rules taught by men" (Isa. 29:13) which, as we have seen before, is the origin of dead traditions and formalism.

(iv) Don't offer unspiritual counsel. One danger we face in this respect is that merely out of our experience we can have something to say in every situation, whether or not what we say is worth saying. Professional talkers, especially in pastoral ministry, need to guard against the temptation to dispense advice to all and sundry or to have an opinion about every topic. That is not true admonition. Unless our admonition rests on the flow of light and truth coming both from the Bible and the Spirit, we shall rush in where even angels fear to tread and become interfering busybodies rather than pastoral counsellors. True counsel relies on the gifts of the Holy Spirit. Sometimes we shall need to keep our counsel and to allow the Holy Spirit Himself to guide into all truth. We shall know when to stand back from a believer who is entering a time of testing, knowing that only our prayers not our prescriptions will see him through.

Teaching everyone with all wisdom

The third form taken by the ministry of the Word in bringing Christians to maturity is "*teaching*". For a full Christian experience the Acts of the Apostles needs to be supplemented by the epistles of the apostles! Continuing "steadfastly in the apostles' teaching" is the sure way to grow. Here again the theme is the same. "Day after day, in the temple courts and from house to house, they never stopped teaching and proclaiming the good news that Jesus is the Christ" (Acts 5:42). At a large celebration gathering, it is Christ who is proclaimed. When a group of disciples meet in a home they are "put in mind of Christ" by scriptural admonition. In the teaching sessions of the Church, it is no different; it is Christ who is the subject of the instructions.

Perhaps we may say this of the characteristics of New Testament teaching.

(i) To teach Christ is to teach *the Truth*. The gospel is the "word of truth" which God desires all men to know and which sets men free (Col. 1:5; 1 Tim. 2:3; John 8:32). Truth, not sensations, brings liberation and builds maturity. Truth embraces true doctrine and genuine experience. It is a beautiful word. To the Greeks "*aletheia*" suggests "reality". In the Old Testament "truth" is always associated with the steadfastness and faithfulness and veracity of God Himself. To attempt to define it is difficult. "Truth is reliable reality", is perhaps the nearest I can get to it. The world certainly needs reality it can rely on. The root cause of the corrupt society so graphically described by Paul when writing to the Romans is that it has "exchanged the truth of God for a lie" (Rom. 1:25). The devil, though neither everywhere-present, nor all-knowing, exercises such widespread influence as the father of lies because he has conned the world into substituting false gods for reality. This is why we are called so clearly to be ministers of revealed truth and why renewal of the mind is so vital a part of Christian maturity. Believers need to be taught clearly what God has accomplished for them in the atonement of His Son, what provisions are now available to them as a result, what strength and life is theirs in union with the glorified and interceding Christ on the throne of God, what the Spirit is doing for them and in them, and what is the nature of the warfare they are called to wage until Christ returns. All this is "the truth that is in Jesus" (Eph. 4:21).

(ii) Truth can be taught effectively only with the power of the Holy Spirit who is *the Spirit of truth*. The anointing that abides upon us is to teach us all things. We impart spiritual truth to spiritual minds because the Spirit of God has brought wisdom from the depths of God to the depths of our own personality and understanding. "We have not received the spirit of the world but the Spirit who is from God, that we may understand what God has freely given us. This is what we speak, not in words taught us by human wisdom but in words taught by the Spirit, expressing spiritual truth in spiritual words" (1 Cor. 2:12–13).

(iii) To teach the truth we must *combat error* and untruth. The apostles knew the positive value of being negative. Every apostle was concerned that the churches knew the truth, not in order to prove their orthodoxy but in order to know how to live godly and wholesome lives. If you believe wrongly, you live wrongly. The Colossians had drifted away from the truth of fullness in Jesus and had fallen for fancy speculation and specious philosophy. Paul gives this new thinking no quarter. Where he finds some Christians hanging onto old traditions of what should or should not be eaten and drunk, Paul goes on the offensive in his teaching. All forms of asceticism, ritualism and legalism must be rejected, he argues, because they lead to bondage and keep Christians in a spiritual babyhood. The pseudo-spirituality that puffs itself up with dreams and visions, private revelations and superior guidance and which is not unknown in charismatic circles, Paul combats relentlessly as unrelated to the Incarnate Christ, to His Body and therefore to real living in it. So Paul teaches the humanity and glory of Jesus and roots all spirituality firmly in the reality of what He is.

(iv) Truth must be taught as a *pattern of teaching*. "But thanks be to God that, though you used to be slaves to sin, you wholeheartedly obeyed the form of teaching to which you were entrusted" (Rom. 6:17). True apostolic teaching is never random or arbitrary, but takes a definite and consistent shape. Christians mature because somewhere in the life of the Church there is a form of teaching which is not optional but to which they are committed by virtue of their commitment to Christ in His Body. Thankfully in the current renewal of the Church, Bible studies no longer exist just to tickle the ears of over-fed saints. God wants to write His laws of truth on our hearts.

(v) Apostolic teaching regularly *recalls Christians to first principles*. Frequently in the New Testament letters appeal is made to Christian beginnings as the ground of further exhortation. Are there difficulties hindering you progressing as believers? Let's go back to what happened when you were baptised into Christ. Did you die with Christ? Were you raised with Christ? How then can you go on sinning? This is a characteristically Pauline argument (Rom. 6:1ff.; Col. 2:12ff.). All this lays stress on how important it is to have a radical and drastic start to the Christian life. Sadly some people pass through commitment classes in a very mechanical and heartless way. What emerges is like forced rhubarb which, though alive, is also limp, rubbery and tasteless! Paul wants the Colossians to go on in the same way they started. "So then, just as you received Christ Jesus as Lord, continue to live in him" (Col. 2:6). You started in freedom, Paul reminds the Galatians, why go on in any other way and lapse into bondage? (Gal. 3:1; 5:1–7). The problem the writer to the Hebrews faces is just this; that he cannot take his readers on to maturity as he would wish because their grounding in the foundation doctrines is so uncertain. Christians who by now ought themselves to be in a position to teach others are still in need of instruction in the ABC of the gospel. To counteract this we will need, from the beginning, as the apostles did, to spell out the consequences of our union with Christ.

(vi) Teaching for maturity will *relate doctrine to life*. The apostles draw the most practical consequences from the most exalted doctrines. The opening section of most New Testament letters is often classed as "doctrinal" and is separated from what is known as the "ethical" passages with which they usually conclude. But true New Testament teaching makes a vital connection between theology and behaviour. Proclaiming Christ as central to all the purposes of God in redemption and history the apostles then usually go on to draw out the immensely practical implications of knowing this for the everyday life of believers. The word "therefore" is the verbal hinge on which this life-giving logic turns. As someone has said, we need to teach what the "therefore" is there for! Christian behaviour is not an arbitrary, irrational set of rules but the outflow of gospel truth. Because Christians have put on Christ in all His majesty and love, they can be expected to put off unforgiveness, lying and bitterness and to put on love, forgiveness and truthful speech. To teach this is to instruct everyone in all the ways of wisdom, which is true "know-how". In this way those we are leading will learn how to behave in the household of God and grow to maturity in Christ. The teacher's aim will be to bring disciples to "full assurance", to that freedom of mind and confidence that results from understanding Christ (Col. 2:2), to the place where they are bold in worship and prayer, secure in who they are in the world and living faithfully and joyfully to the glory of God.

To achieve this will require of the pastor–teacher two things. It will take a lot of *perspiration*. "I want you to know how much I am struggling for you" Paul confesses to the Colossians (2:1). The pressure of hard work and the demands of intercession tax the resources of every shepherd and show us that the teacher's ministry is not for the faint-hearted. It will also need great *inspiration* if, as teachers, we are not to be hampered by reliance on our meagre natural resources and gifts but are to learn to draw on the "energy, which so powerfully works" in us (cf. Col. 1:29).

All this – whether proclamation, admonition or teaching – seems an impossible task. And it is. For as preachers and instructors and teachers of God's Word we are attempting to state the unstateable. But state it we must for there is no other way. When asked why she was a ballerina Pavlova is alleged to have replied: "Do you think I would have danced if I could have told you?"

CHAPTER TWENTY-TWO

Coach

A sporting coach has a key role especially in team games. It is his job to rouse each team-member to play with total commitment. He will try to get the team to play together and with real purpose. He helps each individual to fulfil his potential and to fit into the overall pattern of play. He fires his team to perform with that special "plus" which is more than the sum of its individual talents. Through its coach a team learns to overcome negative thinking and to become success-minded. With a top coach a team begins to believe it can win and therefore usually does.

Nehemiah is a good biblical example of a leader who performed this kind of role for the people of God. Returning home from the Exile with a God-given plan to rebuild the ruined Jerusalem, Nehemiah wisely does not immediately disclose his plans to anyone. Only after careful survey of the job to be done and having armed himself with facts to support his plan does he speak to the people. His first task is to raise their morale and to stir them to action. He soon convinces them of his dream and its practicality. Before long they are as enthusiastic as he is. "Let's build the wall" is now their common aim. Nehemiah assures them of success.

Then he organises them for the task in hand, allotting various jobs to different groups and making sure each one has the resources they need. Once the work has started, he urges them on despite discouragement. He keeps them at it even when they are afflicted by self-doubt and voices are raised to point out how ridiculous the whole enterprise looks! He acts quickly to settle disputes which destroy unity and slow down the work. Constantly he motivates them to keep together and to allow nothing to divert them from their God-given priority. So they built the wall, in 52 days!

Purpose-driven

It is significant to see what Paul was after as he planned to visit the church in Rome. Writing to the Christians there, he tells them what his aims are in coming to them.

- He will make sure that everyone is totally committed. The aim of his apostleship, he says, is "to bring about obedience" in the lives of those he ministers to (Rom. 1:5).

- He will equip them with whatever they need. "I long to see you that I may impart to you some spiritual gift to make you strong" (1:11).

- He will motivate them. He wants to see them so that he and they "may be mutually encouraged by each other's faith" (1:12). In motivating them, of course, he will be stimulated himself.

- He wants to see results from working with them. "I planned to come ... so that I could work among you and see good results" (1:13, LB).

Apostles, prophets, evangelists, pastors and teachers are the basic enabling gifts in the Church. They are given by the ascended Christ to "prepare God's people for works of service" (Eph. 4:12). Another version speaks of the fivefold ministries as given "for the equipping of the saints" (NASB). The Greek word translated "equip" or "prepare" is the word "*katartizo*". It is an interesting word with a variety of uses.

(i) "*Katartizo*" is used of *repairing what is broken*. In medical writings it is used of "*setting broken bones*". Apostles, prophets, evangelists, pastors and teachers maintain the hidden framework on which the Body of Christ is hung. They are concerned for the vital bone structure of the Church – for its doctrine, its vision, its reason for living, its discipline and good order. They seek to repair whatever is out of joint which makes the Church unable to bear the weight of growth. They enable the Church to stand on its feet. "*Katartizo*" is also used of "*mending broken nets*" (Mark 1:19). So the fivefold ministries seek to repair any breaches in love and fellowship within the Church. Tangled or broken nets allow new fish to slip through and be lost. Evangelists have often been thwarted by bad churchmanship. The apostles for their part are eager to untie knots in relationships. "I plead with Euodia and Syntyche to agree with each other in the Lord" (Phil. 4:2). So Paul urges the Corinthians to be "*perfectly united*" ("*katartizo*" 1 Cor. 1:10).

All the ministries devote much time to exhorting believers to "love one another". Each believer is to *"restore"* (*"katartizo"* Gal. 6:1) the erring fellow-Christian to full fellowship. Mending brokenness in individual lives, the ministries bring wholeness to the Church and thus make it fit for its ministry in the world. This kind of leadership eliminates shoddiness and trains the Church for quality work in God's kingdom.

By the grace God has given me, I laid a foundation as an expert builder, and someone else is building on it. But each one should be careful how he builds. For no-one can lay any foundation other than the one already laid, which is Jesus Christ. If any man builds on this foundation using gold, silver, costly stones, wood, hay or straw, his work will be shown for what it is, because the Day will bring it to light. It will be revealed with fire, and the fire will test the quality of each man's work. If what he has built survives, he will receive his reward. If it is burned up, he will suffer loss; he himself will be saved, but only as one escaping through the flames. (1 Cor. 3:10–15)

Making bees sting

It is said that you couldn't motivate a bee to sting if it didn't have the equipment. Fortunately, neither the Church nor its leadership is limited to natural abilities.

(ii) *Katartizo* means *"to supply a lack"*. Paul and his apostolic team of varied ministries are in no doubt about their intentions in visiting the Thessalonian church. "Night and day we pray most earnestly that we may see you again and *supply* [*katartizo*] what is lacking in your faith" 1 Thess. 3:10). Their deficiencies are in doctrine where they need wisdom about the second coming; in pastoral care where they are urged to love even more and to help the weak and timid; in behaviour where they need instruction in righteousness and sexual purity; in evangelistic awareness where some of them are so work-shy as to lose the respect of outsiders; in prophetic understanding where they need teaching on how to use the prophetic gift in the Body. The ministry team led by Paul aims to meet these needs when it comes and writes about them in advance. In a similar way we saw that Paul desired to visit the church in Rome in order to impart some spiritual gift. The Acts of the Apostles reveals the apostles making good various deficiencies in the churches. In Samaria where the evangelist has been unsuccessful, the apostles make good the lack of the baptism in the Holy Spirit by laying hands on the new believers (Acts 8). Paul does a similar thing in Ephesus. Exposing the converts' needs, he fills in what is missing in their experience of the Holy Spirit (Acts 19). Such leaders help members of the Body of Christ to know their gifts and calling, so that unused potential is identified and released. People are sometimes poor judges of themselves and need to be shown what they are really capable of.

So Paul who had been instrumental in equipping Timothy with the spiritual gifts needed for his work, later urges him not to neglect it but to stir it up and use it. Certain skills are taught and gifts given by the ministries, so that, grounded in the Scriptures, each "man of God may be thoroughly equipped for every good work" (2 Tim. 3:17; cf. Heb. 13:21).

(iii) *Katartizo* implies *putting things into order and arrangement*. This is the likely shade of meaning in Hebrews 11:3 where the world is said to have been "formed at God's command" as a cosmos not chaos. It is the task of the enabling ministries to help believers find their place, know their gift and discover their ministry in the Body of Christ. They seek to bring the best out of each member of the Body. "The purposes of a man's heart are deep waters, but a man of understanding draws them out" (Prov. 20:5). Such ministries will be as concerned to see the Church set in order as Paul was when he told Titus what to do in the churches in Crete. "The reason I left you in Crete was that you might straighten out what was left unfinished and appoint elders in every town, as I directed you" (Tit. 1:5). As we have already noted, Paul stated that one of his aims was to bring about obedience in the church he visited. Without the enabling ministries the Church will remain flabby and have as many fringe members as front members. But this will blunt its effectiveness in the world. So the enabling ministries aim for total commitment. They will be concerned in the same way to bring about a right relationship between leaders and led, between teachers and disciples. It is interesting that our word *katartizo* is used in a statement of the Lord Jesus to this effect. "A student is not above his teacher, but everyone who is *fully trained* [*katartizo*] will be like his teacher" (Luke 6:40). This means that spiritual progress has much to do with the relationship between the teacher and disciple and that the disciple's rate of growth depends largely on having a right and submissive attitude towards the teacher.

The ministries of those sent out to equip the Church will also be seeking to bring about *a wise adaptation of part to part* by maintaining the unity of the Church. Having a gift, you do not aim to compete with me but to complement me. So with Christ as Head, "the whole body, joined and held together by every supporting ligament, grows and builds itself up in love, as each part does its work" (Eph. 4:16). As "praise is *ordained* [*katartizo*] from the lips of children and infants", so harmony is achieved in the Body of Christ. The ministries sent to equip the Church are not the composers of the music which is the Church's life and witness, but they are its arrangers. By this arrangement of the music, all the members are able to express themselves fully and at the same time, by submitting to one another, to make symphonies not solos.

In all these ways the ministry gifts of Christ equip His Church to do its work in the world. The "wise adaptation of part to part" is never at the expense of the wise adaptation of "the whole to its purpose". In Howard Snyder's words "the church's task is not to keep Christians off the streets but to send them out equipped for kingdom tasks".[1] *Katartizo* carries with it the idea of effectiveness and efficiency for a result to be achieved. The equipment of the saints is for their work of ministry, for adult work in an adult world. This relative "perfecting of the saints" is for the benefit of the world. So apostles make the Church apostolic, stirring the Church to be outgoing and sacrificial in its lifestyle. Prophets make the Church prophetic, a radical demonstration in word and deed, in song and purity, of what the living God is now saying and doing. Evangelists too, act first on the Body before they act on the world. They aim to make the Church evangelistic, with a heart for the lost, with good news to gossip and healing signs to follow the Word. Pastors are there to make the Church a caring community, where truth is spoken but in love. Teachers make disciples in the

Church, who are instructed in the ways of God, are apt to teach and able to give a joyful reason for the hope within them. The Father took immense care in preparing a body in which His Son could enter the world (Heb. 10:5 – "prepared" = "*katartizo*"). The Son Himself for His part sends to us His ministry of gifts of apostles, prophets, evangelists, pastors and teachers. He sends them so that with equal care and zeal they might "prepare" His spiritual Body to be His means of self-expression on the world.

Moving mountaineers

Most of a coach's work is done from behind the scenes in careful and thorough preparation, increasingly with the help of sports' psychologists. The battle is likewise in the mind with many Christians. To equip the Church for its ministry will be to motivate people to faith. Effective leaders are good motivators. Moving mountains takes faith. But moving mountains is one thing; moving mountaineers is quite another! Such a ministry, like W.H. Auden's poet, will "still persuade us to rejoice" even when the going gets rough. The coach is not an armchair observer, but is usually to be found with tracksuit on, someone to whom "*paraclesis*" is second nature, who loves to get alongside people and urge them on. In so doing such leaders will not only tell us to "run in such a way as to get the prize" but will convince us by their faith and example that we can.

Notes

1. Howard Snyder, *New Wineskins* (London: Marshalls, 1977), p.115.

CHAPTER TWENTY-THREE

Troubleshooter

Apart from being the only living person ever portrayed by John Wayne in a movie, Paul "Red" Adair has another claim to fame. He was the world's greatest expert at fighting oil-well fires. The methods he used to do this are not superficial, as if the problem could be solved by pouring chemical "water" on troubled oil! Instead, his policy was always to get to the very source of the fire and to cap the well even though it may be torching out flames at over two hundred degrees Fahrenheit. Not surprisingly his insurance premiums were high. But wherever and whatever the "blow-out", "Red" Adair made his name as the troubleshooter most oil-men called on in a crisis.

The Church always has need of its own troubleshooters to resolve its internal difficulties. Paul bemoans the lack of such a one at Corinth. "I say this to shame you. Is it possible that there is nobody among you wise enough to judge a dispute between believers?" (1 Cor. 6:5). A charismatic church, rich in spiritual gifts and exalted in knowledge, nevertheless lacked a wise head mature enough to bring peace and order to a confused and competitive group of immature Christians.

The qualities needed by a troubleshooter among God's people are foreshadowed clearly in Solomon, king of Israel. Daunted by the prospect of ruling the nation, the king is encouraged by the Lord to "ask for whatever you want me to give you" (1 Kings 3:5). Feeling like a small child dwarfed by the greatness of the task and the number of the people, Solomon confesses that "I ... do not know how to carry out my duties" (1 Kings 3:7). What he does know is what he needs from God in order to rule Israel and his request pleases the Lord. "So give your servant a discerning heart to govern your people and to distinguish between right and wrong" (1 Kings 3:9). His prayer was answered in full measure. For "God gave Solomon wisdom and very great insight, and a breadth of understanding as measureless as the sand on the seashore" (1 Kings 4:29).

(i) *Wisdom* is the first gift a ruler needs. This is the ability to apply knowledge to bring practical solutions to human needs. To know what our duties are is one thing: to know *how to* carry them out is another and this is wisdom. Such an ability is a divine gift and much to be prized, especially by Christian leaders. "If any of you lacks wisdom, he should ask God, who gives generously to all ... and it will be given to him" (James 1:5). Cleverly, Solomon placates Hiram, king of Tyre by commissioning him to provide raw materials for the new temple he is building. "The Lord gave Solomon wisdom, just as he had promised him. There were peaceful relations between Hiram and Solomon, and the two of them made a treaty" (1 Kings 5:12). The scope of the king's new-found wisdom is amazing. "He spoke three thousand proverbs and his songs numbered a thousand and five" (4:32). So adept did Solomon become at unravelling the complexities of everyday life that his words of wisdom became proverbial, greater than the folklore of the East, greater even than the wise sayings of Egypt to which they bear a superficial resemblance (4:30). Truly the "words of the wise are like goads, their collected sayings, like firmly embedded nails – given by one Shepherd" (Eccl. 12:11).

(ii) *Discernment* is also needed to rule well. Solomon's first test as a troubleshooter was a big one. Two women brought a baby to him and with it a terrible dilemma. Within a short space of time each of them had given birth to a boy. One child however had soon died. His mother then secretly swapped the dead baby for her friend's living one. The mother of the surviving child, initially suspicious, had become convinced that a substitution had taken place. Now, arguing bitterly over who was the true mother of the living child, they stood before Solomon to await his judgement. "Cut the living child in two and give half to one and half to the other" is the king's ruling! "Yes!" agreed the false mother, "neither I nor you shall have him." "Please my lord, give her the living baby!" pleaded the real mother. "Don't kill him!" (1 Kings 3:16–28). For this discernment which distinguished truth from falsehood, Solomon was held in awe by the people. Able to make such practical distinctions to settle disputes Solomon had no difficulty in distinguishing the natural from the spiritual, the temple he was building from the real dwelling place of God (1 Kings 8:27). What is displayed here is the insight which gets beneath the surface to the underlying issues at stake. What Solomon had was a "hearing heart" not just a listening ear. He could pick up the reasons of the heart as well as the arguments of the mouth. People say: "You have understood me", when we have guessed what it is they wanted to say but could not bring themselves to put into words.

(iii) *Breadth of mind* is a God-given asset in a ruler. A troubleshooter cannot afford to be small-minded, unable to see the wood for the trees. Faced with a dispute or unresolved issue, a sense of proportion and perspective is required on the part of the troubleshooter. What is needed is not a narrow specialist but someone able to trace the ways of God wherever they need to be found on the map of life. Solomon's interests were broad. "He described plant life, from the cedar of Lebanon to the hyssop that grows out of walls. He also taught about animals and birds, reptiles and fish" (1 Kings 4:33). In applying the knowledge of God to the various predicaments of everyday living Solomon can ransack creation for parallels and parables. Speech patterns, family relationships, money matters, business affairs, eating and drinking, laughter and tears, love and laziness – all come within the scope of his wise judgement. For all of these areas there is a natural picture or analogy. Lions, sparrows, horses, dogs, ants, badgers, rabbits, locusts and lizards have their lessons for us. So, too, do clouds without rain, babbling brooks, deep water and snow in summer. The way iron sharpens iron, the way butter is churned, the way water reflects a face, the way a bad tooth can't be bitten on – all these yield wisdom for those willing to learn. This breadth of mind makes Solomon a prophet, enabling him to envisage the incoming of the Gentiles to the house of God (1 Kings 8:41ff.). Further qualities which a troubleshooter needs are brought to light in Deuteronomy chapter 1.

Judgements in the household of God

On the verge of the promised land, Moses reminds the children of Israel how at one time they had proved too heavy a burden for him to carry alone. Moses recalls his feelings at the time. "How can I bear your problems and your burdens and your disputes all by myself?" (Deut. 1:12). As we noted in an earlier chapter, Moses decided to delegate responsibility to other wise and understanding leaders respected by the people. He made clear what he expected of them.

(iv) *Impartiality* is essential in troubleshooters. "Do not show partiality in judging" (Deut. 1:17). They will be fair at all times and with all kinds of people. They will be wise enough not to jump to conclusions, bringing no judgement without hearing both sides. Solomon had a word for it: "He who answers before listening – that is his folly and his shame ... The first to present his case seems right, till another comes forward and questions him" (Prov. 18:13,17). He will not judge without making a "thorough investigation" (Deut. 19:18; cf. 21:2). Throughout the Scriptures, partial judges are an abomination (cf. Prov. 24:13).

Even between believers and unbelievers justice must be seen to be done (Deut. 1:16). Once I was visited by a deputation of neighbours complaining about the behaviour of the children of one of our members. On this occasion my judgement was that they were right and I took steps to remedy the situation. I was moved to think that I might be regarded as wise enough to settle a dispute in the community; they were somewhat surprised to find that I had taken so impartial a line with them. This incident stirred me to believe that in a society where common justice is becoming harder to find, those who are wise in the kingdom of God might one day become the only arbiters and judges to which a community can give its confidence. In the future, wisdom may be justified by some strange children and evangelism find some unusual new starting points. And all this is only a training ground for the day when we judge angels!

(v) *Courage* is needed. "Do not be afraid of any man" Moses exhorts his judges (Deut. 1:17b). No judgement should be brought, especially to a dispute, which is forced upon us by emotional pressure. On one occasion, as a young pastor, I recall admonishing a church member too rashly, pressed to do it by other people's emotions. "You really must do something about that," I was urged. The fact that I took along a witness who, though trustworthy, did not share my view of the issue did nothing to help resolve it and I lost my man. I decided that from then on I would never react to a situation under the pressure of other people's feelings. If for no other reason a "wise man keeps himself under control" and does not give "full vent to his anger" (Prov. 29:11). Remaining aloof from threats or inducements, however subtle, is simply the wise way of showing that the "judgement belongs to God"

(Deut. 1:17). Knowing the Lord's verdict through Agabus, Paul can hold to it amidst an emotional and sentimental upheaval that might have swayed a lesser man. Here again the "fear of the Lord is the beginning of wisdom".

(vi) *Knowledge of one's limitation* is vital for wisdom. "Bring me any case too hard for you" (Deut. 1:17). Effective conciliators are wise enough to know when they are confronted with something they cannot handle on their own and are humble enough to seek another's help and counsel. Once again plurality comes into its own for, as we have seen, "in abundance of counsellors there is victory". The issue may well be resolved provided I am not too proud to call in others to cope with matters which I am not qualified or competent to deal with. Above all, as we noted earlier, the judgement which is needed belongs to God and fear of Him is the beginning of our wisdom. Knowing this I am relieved of the burden or illusion of thinking I have all the answers. Faced with complex problems or disputes, I will turn to the Lord, seeking the gifts of the Holy Spirit, especially words of wisdom and knowledge. For this reason a true counsellor has a priestly role, which is concerned not so much with solving my problem as with bringing my case into the presence of God for Him to throw His light upon it (cf. Deut. 17:8–9).

We can summarise what has been said so far.

- Be wise, learning how to apply knowledge to practical needs, becoming as familiar with God's ways as His works.

- Be discerning, ready to listen to the unspoken reasons of the heart, sensitive to the fact that even love needs discrimination.

- Be broad in understanding (which is altogether different from being "broad-minded" in the modern sense), never allowing the details to obscure the weightier more important aspects of the law.

- Be disinterested, with no axe to grind except to know the truth and to set people free.

- Be fearless, not by being aggressive but by being immune to the emotional manipulation of other people whether involved or not.

• Be humble, recognising the gifts of others, and most of all remaining dependent on the gifts which only God can give.

The foolishness of wisdom

Anyone who makes mistakes in this area is in good company, though the scene of such failure may be more serious than our own. Gamaliel is such a case in point, as Luke makes clear in the fifth chapter of the Acts of the Apostles. The apostles are being threatened by a Sanhedrin which has lost all pretence at being an even-tempered assembly. "They were furious and wanted to put them to death" is how Luke describes the mood. At this point a Pharisee, named Gamaliel, intervened to quell the rage. His intervention has all the marks of sweet reasonableness and for this reason has often had a good press among Christian commentators. But on closer inspection Gamaliel turns out not to be the model troubleshooter he at first appears to be.

Firstly, he was *wrong in the caution he showed* (Acts 5:34–40). What appears to be masterful diplomacy is, in fact, political expediency born of uncertainty and indecision. "If" and "on the other hand" seem Gamaliel's keynote words. Alexander Maclaren's verdict is not unfair. "How poor a figure this politic ecclesiastic, mostly anxious not to commit himself ... cuts beside the disciples, who had chosen their side, had done with 'ifs' and went away from the Council rejoicing that they were counted worthy to suffer for the name." Maclaren goes on: "Who would not rather be Peter and John with their bleeding backs than Gamaliel sitting soft in his presidential chair, and too cautious to commit himself to an opinion whether the name of Jesus was that of a prophet or a pretender."

In this case "where is the wise man?" is an ironic indictment of the best that unaided human wisdom can do (cf. 1 Cor. 1:20).

Secondly, Gamaliel was *wrong in the comparisons he drew* (5:36–37). Theudas and Judas were revolutionaries who flourished around the time Jesus was born. These were limited and patronising parallels to find. They showed that Gamaliel's reaction was not deeply rational, the product of thorough investigation. He did not take the trouble to look any further than weak historical precedent and so he obscured the truth. Both examples of leaders whose movements soon petered out show the underlying hope Gamaliel was entertaining. Like a bad smell, the Early Church would, he hoped, just go away!

Thirdly, he was *wrong in the criterion he used* (5:38–39). His arguments were carnal and ill-become a man of God. Since when have observable success or failure been a reliable guide to the godliness or otherwise of a people or a cause. Gamaliel should have known his own history better than this. Israel's own story gave the lie to his criterion for establishing truth. And the cross and resurrection of course had only recently demolished it altogether. For by the foolishness of dying and rising God had made a mockery of human pretensions and argument. Bonhoeffer may have overstated it when he said that Christianity is "the sanctification of failure" but his words are altogether too true for the kind of glibness shown by Gamaliel to grasp.

Lastly, Gamaliel was *wrong in the conclusion he reached*. "Leave these men alone" was hypocritical counsel when it involved flogging and beating the apostles. Some neutrality this was! It was dangerous counsel too, because leaving the apostles alone was just the invitation they needed to set the whole city ablaze with Jesus. It was impossible counsel to give for how can you remain aloof from Christ and his appointed apostles? Not to be for them is to be against them! As a troubleshooter Gamaliel caused more trouble than he was worth.

Firefighting

As we look now at what it means in practice to be a troubleshooter we may find "Red" Adair a better guide than Gamaliel. If as leaders we have any responsibility for resolving issues and settling disputes among the people of God, we need to follow certain guidelines.

(i) *Act promptly.* "There's one thing about any blowout," says "Red" Adair, "they never get better; always worse. So the quicker you can bring them under control, the better off you are." Fear of confrontation here only allows the situation to deteriorate. Attitudes harden and angry words settle into final arguments which everyone is too proud to retract.

(ii) *Treat each case differently.* The troubleshooter in the oil business has a warehouse full of standard firefighting equipment but he knows that each well has its own personality. Spiritual troubleshooters similarly will not pre-judge the issue, bringing to it fixed solutions. They will want to respond flexibly in a way that is appropriate to the person or occasion. Dealing with unreasonable people is an art. Answer a fool according to his folly and you make yourself like him. Yet it may well be right on another occasion to "answer a fool according to his folly, or he will be wise in his own eyes" (Prov. 26:4–5; cf. 2 Cor. 11:16, 12:11). David was wise enough not to presume that he had found a guaranteed method of victory (2 Sam. 1:5). Asking the Lord a second time saved him from the disaster which preconceived ideas would have brought upon him. Direct assault brought victory the first time; but next time it was an encirclement which was the winning tactic.

(iii) *Be prepared to be vulnerable.* "Red" Adair's team once tried to use asbestos clothing to protect them when close to the fire. They soon discarded it because though very protective it proved to be too bulky to work in. Standard psychiatry has long advocated that the counsellor be dispassionate in front of his client, adopting a neutral emotional and moral stance towards him. By contrast, Christian leaders with pastoral care at heart who are dealing with trouble will scarcely want to remain clinical and aloof. They will help to take the heat out of a situation by taking some of it on themselves. "Who is weak, and I do not feel weak? Who is led into sin and I do not inwardly burn?" (2 Cor. 11:29). Firefighters sometimes have to use explosives to clear away damaged surface equipment which is blocking the way to the source of the blowout. Initially a spiritual leader may have to use strong words and take drastic action to take hold of the situation before it gets out of hand. Sharp rebuke may be necessary to disperse the surface emotions and to bring the wranglers to a place where they are calm enough to discuss the real problems. Paul was not afraid to read the riot act to the Corinthians – even if it was "in love".

(iv) *Treat problems as opportunities.* Acts 6 is a striking example of the creative uses to which disagreement can be put! What began in grumbling and dissension was resolved in a way that led to a fresh recognition of the gifts in the Body of Christ and a major new apostolic thrust. In dealing with oil-well blowouts one method used is to dig relief wells some distance away to take the pressure off the main well which has blown. As in Acts 6 we can often take the pressure off by providing other and more godly outlets for the frustration or enthusiasm that has erupted. Locking a person up to their "problem" is usually self-defeating. Finding another way for that person's gifts and zeal to be used – even while still dealing with their problem – usually helps resolve the issue.

(v) *Cover the whole situation with love and patience.* Oil-well blowouts are finally sealed by liquid mud and cement being poured into them. Blowouts in the Church are finally resolved by love and much persistence. This is the love which covers a multitude of sins not by condoning them, but by nullifying their effects especially on others not involved in them.

My own record as a troubleshooter has been patchy. But on one occasion, as a young pastor, I was nearer to success than on others. Returning in euphoria from a particularly stimulating conference, I found a message telling me of a major blowout at one of our house groups in which two men, one of them the leader, had had a violent public disagreement. Immediately, though it was late in the evening, I telephoned the two men involved. I took charge of the situation, told them to "cool it" and arranged to meet them at the earliest opportunity. I first saw each man separately. Then I sought God for specific wisdom on how to deal with the problem. Then, having received this, I presented to each man written instructions on how he should behave in the house group of God and secured each man's agreement as to the justice and rightness of my counsel. I then showed each man the other's written direction. Then I got them together to accept each other's submission to my counsel and to one another. Prayerfully we committed the matter to God and in the weeks that followed I closely monitored the situation.

More remarkable and far more dramatic is Paul's handling of a serious crisis in the twenty-seventh chapter of the Acts of the Apostles. Luke's stirring account of the shipwreck and survival in which Paul was involved serves as a "parable" of what happens when an apostolic troubleshooter takes charge.

Paul had embarked as a prisoner on an Alexandrian ship bound for Italy with 276 men on board. The ship soon hit bad weather, making "slow headway", "with great difficulty" so that "much time was lost" and "sailing had become dangerous". Paul's advice at this point was rejected by the experts and democratic guidance was sought in a majority vote. Things only got worse. With more hope than judgement, more false assumptions than accurate estimates, more guesses than seamanship, the voyage drifted along. Nearly out of control, the ship was lashed together by ropes, a process known as "frapping". Before long the cargo was jettisoned in a vain attempt to settle for less and make life bearable. Finally, all hope of being saved was abandoned (Acts 27:20). At this point Paul takes charge.

A church making slow headway, having great difficulty, lagging well behind the times, at the whim of expert speculation or democratic guesswork, is in real trouble. Barely able to maintain itself, in danger of falling apart, it tends to jettison the things it once felt to be important as the reason for its living. Settling for less, it hopes merely to survive. Soon it lapses into resigned indifference with no confidence that matters will improve. Apostolic wisdom, though hard to take, will prove to be the only hope at this stage. Paul's first word in the crisis is a pointed admonition, the biggest "I-told-you-so" in history (27:21). Secondly, he brings tremendous encouragement and clear, inspiring prophecy to stem the flow of despair and to restore morale. Then he takes his stand as a man with a vision of God and a purpose from God. Confident in belonging to God, in serving God and in believing God, he is able to master his own fears and to instil confidence in others. He is able even to face the fact that things may have to get worse before they get better! (27:26). Withstanding a sudden outbreak of selfish panic, Paul brings further counsel and prophetic encouragement (27:31–34). He even makes the upper deck an upper room and gives thanks to God by breaking what by now must have been very soggy bread. The ship then sank but not before everyone on board had made it to the safety of the shore.

So, unconcerned that old church-structures are breaking up under him, the prophetic troubleshooter delivers God's people from the old order to fight another day.

Fire-raising

In case our earlier analogy proves misleading, it is worth saying that Christian leaders are not only in the firefighting business, but also in the fire-raising business. In every upsurge of the Spirit's activity, leaders will be faced with abuses and excesses usually from those whose maturity does not match their zeal. We will often have to judge and test and assess what is going on. But we will do this with extreme care, anxious not to "put out the Spirit's fire" (1 Thess. 5:19). As James Denney notes, "a fire smokes most when it is newly kindled. Very likely the smoke gets in the eyes; but the way to get rid of the smoke is not to pour cold water on the fire, but to let it burn itself clear."[1]

In this way the foolishness of God confounds the wisdom of men and the sons of light prove wiser than the sons of this world!

Notes

1. James Denney, *1 and 2 Thessalonians* (London: Hodder & Stoughton, 1892), p.236.

CHAPTER TWENTY-FOUR

Doorkeeper

Some years ago the Catholic charismatic theologian, Steve Clark, outlined three approaches to leadership in the Church. The first he called the *status-orientated* approach. Here the leader is most concerned to maintain the order and stability of the organisation. He devotes his energies to preserving the traditions of the institution he serves, upholding its rites and ceremonies as essential to its life, and safeguarding its laws as vital for its existence.

Challenging this is what Clark called the *functional* approach. Here the stress is not on office or position but on gift and ability. The functional leader is very pragmatic, and goal-orientated. He is concerned most of all with getting a job done. Authority in this category is measured by competence and success. Such a leader tends to be the enemy of tradition and the advocate of change. He subjects everything to rigorous scrutiny with the question uppermost in his mind being "does it work?"

It is worth noting here that in the renewal of the Church by the Holy Spirit there has been a welcome shift from the first type of leadership to the second. Much of what we are saying in this section of the book about the ministries in the Church comes within this functional category. But there is a third approach to leadership according to Clark. This he termed the *environmental* style of leadership. It is to this category, Clark maintains, that the biblical role of the elder belongs.[1]

It is this vital ministry of eldership that I now want to discuss. Clark's suggestion that an elder has an environmental approach to his ministry is a helpful one. An elder:

- is less work-orientated and more "value-orientated"
- gathers people and is concerned for their attitudes.

How do they view one another? How do they value the group? Do they esteem one another? Are they growing in their relationships with one another? These are the questions elders ask of those in their care.

An elder:

- is not pre-occupied with running the church's activities

- does not measure success by how well the church does certain well-defined things

- is interested in its inner health, in the climate or environment in which the members live and which will so radically effect their growth and effectiveness.

The difference between the functional approach and the one we are now describing is a little like that between a production manager and a personnel officer. The former is chiefly concerned for the efficiency of the machinery, the smooth running of the assembly line, the competence and skill of the individual worker and the quality of the product. The latter has the job of looking after the environment in which all this can happen, even becoming involved in sorting out disputes between workers, especially demarcation ones. What matters to the personnel manager are the working conditions in the factory, its heating, lighting and air-conditioning; whether the workers have proper lunch breaks and proper protective clothing; whether they have problems in the family or difficulties over pensions or worries about redundancy. These things affect the success of the venture just as much as the skill of each worker or the efficiency of his machine. This is probably far too idealistic in today's rough industrial climate. But in the Church it is not. According to this analysis, an elder seeks to maintain the Body as a life-support system for believers. Elders will have a "feel" for the flow of life in the Body of Christ, for how the Body works and for how each individual is contributing to its atmosphere and climate.

Eldership has Old Testament roots which are worth considering. Originally elders were the heads of families, later called together as the representatives of Israel (Exod. 12:21ff.; 18:1ff.). Later, we are told, they "sat in the gate" of each city, exercising a judicial and governmental function. They become "doorkeepers" of each community, the regulators of its affairs, its effective and collective leadership (cf. Deut. 25:7–8; 1 Sam. 16:4; Ruth 4:1ff.). When we come to the New Testament we find the elders in Judaism occupying a strong and prominent role in the opposition to Jesus, and elsewhere as the presidents of local synagogues.

In the Early Church, then, there was precedent for the appointment of elders as the local leaders of the gathered community of Christ's people (Acts 11:30; 14:23; 20:17; 21:18). Their role was soon seen as essential if the new groups of believers were to be built up and strengthened. Paul tells Titus that the appointment of elders in the places he is sent to is part of the setting in order of the churches without which they would be in an "unfinished" state (Titus 1:5: "that you might straighten out what was left unfinished"). Significantly, too, elders are mentioned in the plural in almost every case. Together they act as the leaders of local churches.

Overseen not overlooked

There is another term which in the New Testament is used synony-mously with "elder" ("*presbuteros*"). This is the word "overseer" or "bishop" ("*episkopos*"). Since the research of J.B. Lightfoot it has been generally accepted that both these terms refer to the same man and the same role. "Overseer" has more of a Greek history than "elder" though it, too, can be traced in the Old Testament. In the Greek Old Testament "*episkopos*" is used of Eleazer who had "oversight" of the tabernacle (Num. 4:16 LXX). Since it is God who has "oversight" of the whole land, with His eyes continually on it, "*episkopoi*" are His delegates who take care of what He cares for (cf. Deut. 11:12). God "looks out" a people for Himself; overseers are delegated to "look after" them.

It is ironic that in current English, "oversight" has come to mean the exact opposite of what it originally meant. Now it means "failure to notice or pay attention to" and implies indifference and neglect! This usage is as far as could be from the early meaning of "*episkopos*" which means one who takes care of others, who watches over them, looks after them. It is this supervision that is truly biblical. Incidentally, it is worth, at this point, countering another misunderstanding of "over-sight". If it does not mean "overlook", then equally it does not mean "look over" as if it implied "looking over someone's shoulder" in a threatening and oppressive way.

Some leadership sends out the Orwellian signal that "Big Brother is watching you and really loves you!"

Being before doing

Though "elder" and "overseer" are used synonymously in the New Testament, it has been suggested that "elder" refers to what a local leader *is*, while "overseer" refers to what they *do*. Whether this distinction is true or not, what is clear is that the apostles set great store by the qualities of character which qualify people to be elders of the Church.

In the Pastoral Epistles, eldership still seems tied to family headship and appears for the most part to be a male function. Paul tells Timothy that a measure of maturity is the best recommendation for eldership. Is the candidate morally reliable? Little stress is laid at this point on a prospective elder's gifts apart from being able to rule and apt to teach. The qualities listed by the apostle in writing to Timothy and Titus are to be seen less as legal requirements than as clear counsel to both men on what to look for in potential elders. Basically eldership must qualify on two counts: *self-management* ("temperate, self-controlled ... not violent, but gentle ... upright, holy and disciplined", 1 Tim. 3:1ff.; Titus 1:6ff.) and *domestic management* ("husband of but one wife, a man whose children believe and are not open to the charge of being wild and disobedient", Titus 1:6) for "if anyone does not know how to manage his own family, how can he take care of God's church" (1 Tim. 3:5). So the stress is on character rather than on charisma. Because elders operate in a given locality where people know them well, they must have a "good reputation with outsiders" so as not to fall into disgrace (1 Tim. 3:7). But immersed as they are in the affairs of the local church they must not become parochial or lose a vision for the wider Church and its calling in the world. Committed to plurality they must be able to work with others in mutual submission as together they seek the will of God for the Church.

Elders are not, therefore, to be autocratic managers of the people; not academic teachers nor even all specialised counsellors. Nor should any elder be a representative or delegate of some sectional interest in the

Church. To be an elder is to be a guardian, an overseer, a shepherd of the whole flock, who watches over the sheep, succours the weak and is alert to what threatens them (cf. Acts 20:11, 28, 21, 35). The elder, in short, exercises a clear pastoral ministry.

There is no job description of eldership given in the New Testament but there are fleeting glimpses of their work. They "stand in front of others", are able to keep control, to manage, to take care of others. Elders rule, in the sense of seeking to implement heaven's rule on earth. Like their heavenly counterparts, they rule best when they are worshippers, at home in the throne room of God. Those who "rule well" can expect financial reward (1 Tim. 5:17). Such is their respect that elders are protected from trivial complaints made against them (1 Tim. 5:19). Such is the responsibility of eldership that its judgement is made public (1 Tim. 5:20). Eldership exercises oversight of the Church's money which is perhaps why it is warned against greed and urged to exemplify scrupulous honesty (1 Tim. 3:3; Titus 1:7; 1 Pet. 5:2). With the example of the "overseer" Judas in mind this is timely wisdom for elders (cf. Acts 1:20). Elders help to maintain church discipline which is perhaps why they must not be quick-tempered or overbearing (Titus 1:7–8; 1 Pet. 5:3). They need to be compassionate with strong faith, able to be called upon to heal the sick (James 5:14). Although not always a full-scale teacher, an elder must nonetheless "hold firmly to the trustworthy message as it has been taught, so that he can encourage others by sound doctrine and refute those who oppose it" (Titus 1:9).

All this is enough to confirm that "If anyone sets his heart on being an overseer, he desires a noble work" (1 Tim. 3:1). The fact that eldership is made by the Holy Spirit and is appointed only in concert with apostolic ministry gives each church initial and additional confidence that it has got the right person (Acts 14:23; Titus 1:5). This practice is a safeguard for a local church against the abuse of eldership, giving it the right of appeal to other wisdom in the Church, and protecting it from self-appointed, self-perpetuating local leaders. In fact this three-way relationship between a local church, its elders and the apostles, is a vital one and is fast becoming a live issue in the Church today.

Open doors

As the doorkeeper of the flock of God, the elder is obviously responsible for *closing the door* to false teachers and prophets who seek to
infiltrate the local church. "I know that after I leave," Paul warned the
Ephesian elders, "savage wolves will come in among you and will not
spare the flock" (Acts 20:29). Equally, an elder must *keep the door open*
for genuine and God-sent trans-local ministries. It was tension
between local and trans-local ministries which led the apostle John to
write with some grief to his friend Gaius. In what we know as his third
letter, John is concerned to deal with the trouble caused to a local
church by a man called Diotrephes. This man, it appears, "loves to be
first" and has arrogated to himself the leadership of the church. He is
clearly proud, unsubmissive, seeking to exercise authority without
being under it, and overbearing to those beneath him in his care. What
is most damaging to the church is his attitude to the apostle John (3
John 9). Diotrephes is closing the door to outside ministry and is rejecting apostolic covering and input. In doing so he deprives the church
of the benefits of the other travelling ministries by refusing to welcome
travelling missionary and Christian messengers (3 John 10).

From this vivid glimpse of first-century problems, there emerges a very
important principle. A local elder needs to open the door of the church
to other gifts of ministry. Too many local elders are still shutting out
the apostles, prophets, pastors, teachers and evangelists whom the
Risen Christ is giving to enrich and equip the whole of His Church. But
an eldership which takes this course locks the people into its own
limited gifts and leadership. It risks becoming authoritarian, like
Diotrephes. Either way the local church will lose something of the fullness of Christ which is in store for them.

Is this why it is so often urged that an elder should be "hospitable" (1
Tim. 3:2; Titus 1:8)? There is more to this than meets the eye once we
understand first-century conditions Church life. The Church, in Sir
William Ramsey's words, could not expose its members, whether jour-
neying on public or private errands "to the corrupt and nauseous sur-
roundings of the inns kept by persons of the worst class in existing
society".[2] And not only the safety but the strategy of the Church was
furthered by loving hospitality. For such hospitality implied an open

door not only to the saints who arrived on your doorstep but to visiting apostolic delegates and trans-local ministries. Local elders like Diotrephes could make or break this strategy. On such a seemingly insignificant virtue as hospitality depended "the communion of the churches generally, the maintenance of Apostolic authority and of unity in faith amongst them, and the continued propagation of the Gospel".[3] In exercising this spiritual role, it will be said of the true elder, as was said of Eliakim, entrusted with divine authority, that "what he opens no-one can shut, and what he shuts no-one can open" (Isa. 22:22).

Perhaps the best hope for elders is to remember that they are the door-keeper not the door. The Pharisaic leaders of Israel had closed the door to God's kingdom to so many and thrown away the key. Jesus is the Door. An elder's highest privilege is to attend this ever-open Door, to welcome all who come to it, and to encourage them not to linger on the threshold but to enter fully into the joy and facilities of the Father's house.

Notes

1. Steve Clark, *Building Christian Communities* (Notre Dame: Ave Maria Press, 1972).
2. Quoted by G.G. Findlay, *Fellowship in the Life Eternal* (London: Hodder & Stoughton, 1907), p.15.
3. Ibid. p.16.

CHAPTER TWENTY-FIVE

Trailblazer

Four times in the New Testament the term "leader" is applied to the Lord Jesus.

Jesus is

- the leader into life (Acts 3:15)
- the leader in salvation (Acts 5:31)
- the leader to glory (Heb. 2:10)
- the leader of faith (Heb. 12:2).

The Greek word used in these instances is *"archegos"*. As Philip Hughes notes it is a very interesting word but one which is difficult to translate satisfactorily. "It signifies," he writes, "one who is both the source or initiator and the leader, one who takes first action and then brings those on whose behalf he has acted to the intended goal."[1] It carries with it the sense of founder or author, and suggests a certain princeliness as the different versions indicate.

Elsewhere in the letter to the Hebrews, Jesus is called the *"aitios"* of salvation which points to Him as the "personal mediating cause" whose instrumentality makes him the "source" of salvation to others (Heb. 5:9). Jesus is also designated our *"prodromos"* or "forerunner" who like an advance party, has gone on ahead to open up the way for us, in this case into the Holiest (6:20).

To take our cue from Him at this point will give a special colouring to our understanding of leadership. We shall be unable to rest easy in being defenders of the status quo or maintainers of a static institution. The view of Jesus we have sketched implies movement, progress, change and advance in His Church. The kind of leadership appropriate to this will be that which is caught up in His momentum as a pioneer and trailblazer.

The writer to the Hebrews has Old Testament precedent in mind.

Perhaps he is thinking of Joseph who was able to look back on his brothers' rejection as in the will of God. "God sent me *ahead of you* to preserve for you a remnant on earth and to save your lives by a great deliverance" (Gen. 45:7). He may be thinking of the Lord's words to Moses: "Go ... and lead the people on their way, so that they may enter and possess the land ..." (Deut. 10:11). More likely he is finding a parallel to Joshua who was called, as leader, to "*cross over ahead*" of the people (Deut. 31:3f.) – counsel which Joshua himself later passed on to the priests on the verge of the Jordan (Josh. 3:6).

The leader's initiative here consisted in breaking new ground. This was in direct response to the initiatives of God Himself who by fiery pillar and shady cloud "went ahead" of His people to make their way straight. God goes before His people, and the leaders who follow Him and keep pace with Him are the true leaders. Of the spies who went ahead to assess the land it was Joshua and Caleb who were the real trailblazers because they had the faith to follow the Lord without reservation. Defying giants of opposition they seized grapes of opportunity which would benefit and motivate those they were to lead. Adventuring so far ahead of the people they might have been tempted to disappear into the distance, into a privileged and private "promised land" of their own. Leaders with prophetic gift especially need to resist this temptation. Some become so avant-garde as to become elitist, inhabiting a rarified atmosphere, cut off from the needs and aspirations of normal mortals. Flying "Concorde" they tend to arrive before the rest of us have started! Caleb and Joshua were not "high-flyers" but pathfinders for the sake of others. They went further than the people in a spirit of faith, boldness, and prophetic foresight but they returned to where the people were in order to begin the more humdrum and frustratingly slow task of leading others into the good of what they had seen.

Settler or pioneer

The difference between a settler- and a pioneer-mentality has become a familiar one in recent years. Slightly adapted, it clarifies the approach to leadership we are describing. In settler theology, the Church is a courthouse. It is a symbol of security, law and order. In pioneer theology, the

Church is a covered wagon, always on the move, bearing the marks of life and always where the action is. Similarly, in settler theology, a leader is the sheriff, sent to enforce the rules. In pioneer theology, the leader is a scout, riding out ahead to find out which way the other pioneers should go. Trailblazing leadership lives the dangers of the trail and doesn't ask the pioneers to do what it hasn't done first. Its spirit and courage serve as a model for all to follow.

True trailblazing prepares the way for fresh movements of God. In doing this the pioneering leader may have to hack a way through a jungle of traditions and accepted ideas. Doing this will not be, however, to prove "contemporary" or trendy, but in order to bring others on to clear ground. John the Baptist was a true radical, wielding an axe honed to sharpness on the very untrendy stones of repentance and righteousness. There is a faith and forthrightness called for here in spiritual leaders which is the indispensable prerequisite to revival. A pre-emptive strike by the prophets is only to pave the way for new advances in God. An axe needs to be laid at the root of every tree Father has not planted if room is to be made for God to move.

Nearly every major breakthrough in medicine and science has been achieved by pioneers who pressed through to new discoveries. Often ridiculed by a disbelieving world, mocked by patronising colleagues, they persisted in their research. They made mistakes, took risks, but had the passionate determination to break new ground. But, in Peter Marshall's words, "Why are there so few spiritual discoveries to match the progress made by science? The answer lies in lack of researchers. How many are willing to give themselves away to take risks in spiritual research?"[2] Another New Testament word for leadership is *"prohistemi"* which implies *"one who stands in front of others"* (cf. Rom. 12:8; 1 Thess. 5:12). Like an Eastern shepherd such a leader will lead the flock from the front not nag them from behind. This suggests the courage to take initiatives and make decisions.

Heroes

Christians, especially, badly need heroes worth looking up to; and living heroes not just dead ones! It is precisely this lack which true spiritual leadership is intended to supply. The principle of *imitation* in leadership is clear in the New Testament. "Copy me ... as I copy Christ," Paul urges the Corinthians (1 Cor. 11:1, Phillips). "I implore you," Paul exhorts his spiritual family, "to follow the footsteps of me your father" (1 Cor. 4:16, Phillips). "You became imitators of us and of the Lord," he reminds the Thessalonians (1 Thess. 1:6). The "and of the Lord" is a vital qualification and safeguard. It reminds us that while we make a someone our model, we must never make anyone our idol!

Behind this principle of imitation lies a basic strategy. As leaders, we ask others to imitate us because we are called to make disciples. Formation not information is our aim. As leaders, we best achieve this not merely by speaking truth worth trusting but by living lives worth emulating.

Moral authority can make each of us an *example* of what a believer should be (1 Tim. 4:12). Titus, like Timothy, is called to be a "*tupos*", letting his life stand as a pattern for others (Titus 2:7). Trailblazing, far from implying that leaders zoom off into a stratosphere of their own advanced thinking, means that they go before the people in the down-to-earth business of living, of speech, of love, of faith, of purity. Youthful leaders blaze a trail not by being eccentric but by being exemplary. Elders oversee the Church not by being over-bearing, not by acting like "little tin gods" but by being examples to the flock (1 Pet. 5:3, Phillips).

Success breeds success

What this means is that a leader must be *believable*, a credible witness to what he is saying. "The Lord said to Moses, 'I am going to come to you in a dense cloud, so that people will hear me speaking with you and will always put their trust in you' " (Exod. 19:9). To have "faith in the Lord" means to have "faith in his prophets" (2 Chron. 20:20). And what is more, "Have faith in his prophets and you will be successful". Success is not defined by the culture but by God's ways but, nonetheless, leaders who are going somewhere attract followers.

For this reason Paul exhorts Timothy to lead an exemplary life so that *"everyone may see your progress"* (1 Tim. 4:15). If a leader is growing in God, the people are more likely to grow to. If the leader is static they will have nothing to follow. This is more than merely being one step ahead of the people though every leader knows that desperation drives us to this on occasions. The picture of the panic-stricken leader in the bathroom with his open Bible sweating to get a "word" ten minutes before the house group arrives is too familiar to be funny. What Paul is stressing is that leaders who continue to make significant advances in their own Christian life offer something to others to emulate.

Timothy is to be a pattern to the believers by showing them how to live the life in Christ.

(i) To be "Timothy-like" is not to be a critic on the sidelines but someone who walks alongside others, liable, as they are, to make mistakes.

(ii) It is to stir up one's own spiritual gifts. In this way the people of God may be roused from sluggishness and stimulated to rise to their own calling and fulfil their own God-given potential.

(iii) To be "Timothy-like" is to settle on priorities for oneself and the people. Devotion to these things will show the people what to concentrate on. What a leader treats casually will most likely be treated lightly by the people. Whatever a leader is absorbed in they will take seriously.

(iv) This means that, like Timothy, we are called as leaders to begin to live more open lives before the people – however risky this may seem. It is by considering the "outcome" of our "way of life" that others will respect us and come to imitate us (Heb. 13:7). In this it is an encouragement to know that we are expected to be examples not of lives which have reached perfection but of lives lived humbly in the process of becoming like Christ. If, as Timothy was urged, we persevere in this, we will carry others along with us to greater maturity. "Persevere in them, because if you do, you will save both yourself and your hearers" (1 Tim. 4:16).

Do you want a pilot?

The last New Testament term to consider in this chapter is *"kuberne-sis"* which occurs in 1 Corinthians 12:28. "And in the church God has appointed ... those with gifts of *administration.*" It may at first seem strange to be treating administration as a subheading of trailblazing. How do we relate an apparently static picture of a neat and tidy office manager to the more dynamic image of a bold and adventurous trail-blazer? Part of the answer to this is to discard preconceived ideas. I am all for efficient office management but I suspect that there is more to a New Testament administrator than this. *"Kubernesis"* basically means a "steersman" or "pilot" who brings influence to bear to point some-thing in a particular direction. The various translations of this word give their own flavour. It means "good leaders" (JB), those "given the power to direct others" or "to guide them" (TEV, NEB). Barclay para-phrases it as "those with the ability to administer the affairs of the church". J.B. Phillips calls them "organisers" and The Living Bible "those who can get others to work together".

(i) *Overseers* obviously need this ability and they have to receive it from the Holy Spirit. Dr John Hesselink of Western Theological Seminary in Holland, Michigan, wrote of his fears at being invited to become President of the seminary. After thirty years of missionary work, of preaching and teaching during which he had done very little administration, he felt unequipped for the new role he was adopting. "My charismatic friends," he wrote with good humour, "along with others prayed for the healing of my eye when I had a detached retina in the fall of 1980; and I suspect others prayed that I might experience the gift of speaking in tongues. But none, as far as I know, prayed that I might receive the gift of administration or leadership, even though nothing would be more directly beneficial for me, given my present vocation."[3] Dr Hesselink prayed for himself and enjoyed many years of administrative duties with the gifts and graces provided by the Holy Spirit for the task.

(ii) *Pastors* need to recognise this gift in others if they are to promote Body-life. Howard Snyder relates his experience as the missionary pastor of a small church in a growing, working-class community on the edge of the city of Sao Paulo, Brazil. Living twenty miles away on the other side of the city and with many other responsibilities, he was able to visit the church only twice a week. Language and cultural barriers made his administrative oversight even more unsatisfactory. Then he noticed that at planning sessions one brother, Andrew, always took notes on a little pad. Andrew was a recent convert, not well educated, who had been an alcoholic before turning to Christ. "As I got to know Andrew better," recalls Snyder, "I found he had a gift for organisation and administration. He knew how to bring people together around a common purpose and get a job done. He had not learned this anywhere; it seemed to be a gift of grace."[4]

(iii) Even *worship leaders* might aspire to this gift! The ability to steer the flow of charismatic worship is a priceless asset. It is derived both from careful preparation which gives a sense of purpose and an awareness of what the Spirit is doing as He plots His own course among a worshipping community. But then a pilot consults not only maps and chart, but wind, tide and current.

(iv) Most important of all, *growth ministries* need this gift. Given originally in a period of fluid development, it is especially useful as the Church looks to increase and enlarge. The gift of "*kubernesis*" is a vital part of a faith ministry. It provides the practical foresight which can anticipate in vision the consequences of growth and expansion and can begin in faith to make provision for them. It helps to blaze the trail for a new visitation from God. Expanding the base of operations with gifted people may be the prophetic *prelude* rather than the panicky *result* of God-given growth.

This is a far cry from mere office management. A charismatic administrator seeks *the gift of prophetic planning*. Bold initiators, faithful models of adventurous living, pioneers of uncharted realms of the miraculous, frontrunners and forerunners, and those with practical foresight and faith – all these in their own measure are trailblazers, preparing the way of the Lord.

Valour from His eyes

We began by looking at Jesus. He is Leader of the leaders and we fulfil our calling by fixing our gaze on Him. Sometimes what we are saying is less important than the direction in which we are facing. For it is to the Lord Jesus we look for inspiration in leadership.

> I have a captain, and the heart of every private man
> Has drunk in valour from his eyes,
> Since first the war began.
> He is most merciful in fight,
> And of his scars a single sight
> The embers of my failing light
> Into a flame can fan.[5]

In settler theology, sin is breaking one of the town's ordinances. In pioneer theology, sin is wanting to turn back. At the risk of losing a reader or two, I confess my admiration for Edward Irving, that "man ahead of his time" who, though much maligned, was a trailblazer of the Church's renewal and restoration. Of John the Baptist, Irving once wrote:

> It seems to me that the Baptist is a type of every herald of salvation. We have to do with the same over-grown wilderness of moral life. There are the same towers of pride and mountains of vanity to be brought low; the same hollow hopelessness and deep despair to be filled with consolation and assurance; the same rough asperities of character to be shorn smooth; the same crooked and intriguing policies to be made straight, that the gospel of Christ may have free course and be glorified; there is the same gate upon the heart to be lifted up; the same bolted, barred gates have to lift up their hearts, that the King of Glory may enter in.[6]

In pursuit of this goal as leaders and to adapt Unamuno's prayer: "May God deny us peace but give us glory."

Finishing this book closed a chapter earlier in my life. To be a leader is to break new ground for God, for myself and hopefully for others. This I must now do. What we gain by trailblazing is not always apparent. But what we have glimpsed so far we speak of with bated breath and without disillusionment. Perhaps this was how Kipling's "Explorer" felt after he had spied out his "promised land".

Have I named one single river? Have I claimed one single acre?
Have I kept one single nugget – (barring samples)? No, not I!
Because my price was paid me ten times over by my Maker.
But you wouldn't understand it. You go up and occupy.

Ores you'll find there; wood and castle; water-transit sure and steady
(That should keep the railway-rates down), coal and iron at your doors.
God took care to hide that country till He judged His people ready,
Then He chose me for His Whisper, and I've found it, and it's yours!

Endurance is an unfashionable quality in a period when easy answers and instant solutions are expected. But to endure is necessary for all who are still "towards" everything, even in their leadership. Our incentive as leaders is to follow our leader, and "not lose sight of Jesus who leads us in our faith". He endured the cross for the sake of the joy set before Him.

Notes

1. P.E. Hughes, *A Commentary on the Epistle to the Hebrews* (Grand Rapids: Eerdmans, 1977), p.100.
2. Peter Marshall, *Mr Jones, Meet the Master* (New York: Fleming Revell, 1950), p.73.
3. John Hesselink was writing in the magazine *Pastoral Renewal* in September 1982.
4. Howard Snyder, *Liberating the Church* (Basingstoke: Marshalls, 1983), p.254.
5. Thomas Toke Lynch.
6. H.C. Whitley, *Blinded Eagle* (London: SCM, 1955), p.117.

CHAPTER TWENTY-SIX

Starter for 10

Especially for beleaguered leaders, we summarise suggested ways of co-operating with God in effecting biblical changes in the Church.

(i) *Be ready to change yourself*
"You and I are incompatible," said the Lord once to Bob Mumford, "and I don't change." As the man who thought he was stuck in a telephone box discovered after calling the fire brigade – the door opens inwards. Change begins with us. Laying down the shield of professionalism, finding a new sense of identity and security, losing our fear of failure or criticism – these prepare us for leading others into change. Ezekiel was told to groan in the sight of the people. When I show genuine emotion others know I am not a plastic man, unaffected by the need for change urged on them.

(ii) *Be clear about your vision for the Church*
Is it renewal of traditional Church structures which I am after? Do I have a vision of the one Body which God has set His heart on or will I settle for a pepped-up denominationalism? One thing is sure: if my trumpet blows an uncertain sound or my eye is not single the saints become confused and defensive. Where there is no prophetic vision among leaders the people will be scattered, unrestrained and ungovernable (Prov. 29:18). Paying the price of the vision may involve losing much, even a roof over our heads! (Ezek. 12:1ff.). The leader who has nothing to die for has nothing to live for.

(iii) *Repeatedly teach and affirm the biblical basis of the changes that are taking place*
"How dare you tell me how to worship! – I'll worship my way." Such emotional reactions can be effectively withstood only by thorough teaching from the Scriptures on how God wants to be worshipped, so that we may do it His way. In most cases of hostility to change, the Holy Spirit is taking the blame for the radical effect of the Word of God. The apostles used the Old Testament to justify New Testament changes; so must we.

(iv) *Stress the living Word of God*

Saturation preaching has made many evangelical Christians almost immune to the living Word of God. The idea that the Spirit may be saying something to our church about what God wants us to do today, comes as a shock to many. But God's Word in its sword-like thrust penetrates anything we are doing which does not have sound biblical foundations. "Why do your disciples not walk according to the tradition of the Baptists (or Methodists or URC's, etc.) but sing their songs with upraised hands?" Such attitudes face the charge of invalidating the Word of God! Faith comes by hearing (not hearsay!) and hearing by the Word of Christ – not the traditions of men.

(v) *Be committed to all that God wants to do*

Israel was accused of wanting God's work but not His ways (Psa. 95:9–10). So in every time of refreshing we are prone to want the fruits without the obligations inherent in the blessing of God. It is easy to settle for livelier worship with a new song book alongside the hymn book. But we can sing the songs the Holy Spirit has given while keeping the lid shut tightly on His other gifts. The changes He has in mind are more drastic than two "choruses" slipped into the hymn-sandwich, fervently gobbled up by an eager minority and grimly tolerated by the rest! Enjoying the spin-offs of renewal without commitment to the restoration of the Church's structures is not only hypocritical but self-defeating.

(vi) *Lead from the front not behind*

"The people told me to" is a poor excuse for any leader – though both Aaron and Saul tried it (Exod. 32:21ff.; 1 Sam. 15:24). Recall, the Greek "to stand in front of" (Rom. 12:8). Doing it before the Lord who is your audience will release you from self-consciousness – as it did David when he danced before the ark. It will also enable you to bear with criticism or misunderstanding. Meekness only adds to your authority here.

(vii) *Break with the expectations of the people*

Jesus refused to be the Messiah the people wanted (Matt. 11:2; John 6:15). Do not be swamped by the pressures of what people think you should be doing. Listen to God. Jesus even let His best friend die rather than get out of line with Father's timing and plans (John 11:5ff.). Let God give you a flock. You will know who they are because they will hear the Great Shepherd's voice in yours and follow you. Be prepared, therefore, like Gideon, to lose the right people. Some help, as Ezra found, you can do without (Ezra 4:3). "Why can't we have two services?" I was asked once. "One for those who like the old-type service, and one for those who want to do these daft new things." All I could say in reply was to ask who would be leading these alternative services. "You would, of course." To which I could only say that I was doing it the way I felt to be right already. Few organisations are indispensable either. You can start the process of change by refusing to support even as a figurehead any church activity you do not believe in. Bob Girard has put it well: "Anything in the church programme that cannot be maintained without constant pastoral pressure on the people to be involved should be allowed to die a sure and natural death."[1]

(viii) *Make small but significant changes*

The prophets used symbolic actions to implement their word. To refer to this may sound like using a sledgehammer to crack a nut. But it is precisely the small, seemingly unimportant visible changes that most provocatively focus the preaching of the Word. Many who remain unmoved by prophetic preaching get immediately aroused when anyone does something different from the usual. Putting the chairs in a circle, raising the hands, using one loaf and one cup – these actions, among countless others, unimportant in themselves can, nevertheless, be very important in the context of a need to respond to what the "now" Word of the Lord is saying. Thankfully we do not have to go naked for three years, as Isaiah did, or hide our underwear in a ledge in the rock as Jeremiah did, or even lie on one side for three hundred days as Ezekiel did! Our actions, more modest in every way, may nonetheless like those of former prophets, become "actions which under the hand of God initiate a movement of the Divine Spirit in the affairs of men".[2] People will at least know you mean what you say, and so will be challenged to reach to the "now" Word because actual choices confront them.

(ix) *Build relationships with other godly leaders both within and outside the local church*

Make disciples as Jesus did, then what God is saying through you will become established truth and vision, no longer at risk if you get run over by a bus! Instead of your hobbyhorse which hopefully may go away soon, this vision can begin to create an alternative to the existing structures and system. In turn these faithful people – to whom you have committed yourself and your dreams – can teach others, thus eventually bringing the whole Church into clarity and peace. In the same way it is good to get into responsible and regular relationships with other godly leaders in the area. Friends like this, whom you can trust, are an incredible blessing from the Lord. Standing with you, at first privately then later publicly, they will reinforce your own spiritual authority by showing that you too are under authority. In time, we can by this means begin to see more clearly just what we are in God, and come to recognise the apostles, prophets, shepherds, teachers and evangelists whom Jesus is raising up today in His Church.

(x) *Believe your own prophecies*

At the end of *The Hobbit* Gandalf tells the surprised Bilbo that he should not have disbelieved prophecies simply because he himself had uttered them. Nor should we. A sober estimate of ourselves will save us from an inflated idea of our own importance. The Lord we serve, not us, is the author and finisher of our faith. But the joy set before us is no illusion. Why settle for less for the sake of a quiet life.

Notes

1. Bob Girard, *Brethren Hang Loose* (Grand Rapids: Zondervan, 1972), p.73.
2. George A. Knight, *A Theology of the Old Testament* (London: SCM, 1969), p.185.

National Distributors

UK: (and countries not listed below)
CWR, Waverley Abbey House, Waverley Lane, Farnham, Surrey GU9 8EP.
Tel: (01252) 784710 Outside UK: (44) 1252 784710

AUSTRALIA: CMC Australasia, PO Box 519, Belmont, Victoria 3216. Tel: (03) 5241 3288

CANADA: CMC Distribution Ltd, PO Box 7000, Niagara on the Lake, Ontario L0S 1J0.
Tel: 1800 325 1297

GHANA: Challenge Enterprises of Ghana, PO Box 5723, Accra.
Tel: (021) 222437/223249 Fax: (021) 226227

HONG KONG: Cross Communications Ltd, 1/F, 562A Nathan Road, Kowloon.
Tel: 2780 1188 Fax: 2770 6229

INDIA: Crystal Communications, 10-3-18/4/1, East Marredpally, Secunderabad – 500 026.
Tel/Fax: (040) 7732801

KENYA: Keswick Bookshop, PO Box 10242, Nairobi.
Tel: (02) 331692/226047 Fax: (02) 728557

MALAYSIA: Salvation Book Centre (M) Sdn Bhd, 23 Jalan SS 2/64, 47300 Petaling Jaya,
Selangor.
Tel: (03) 78766411/78766797 Fax: (03) 78757066/78756360

NEW ZEALAND: CMC Australasia, PO Box 36015, Lower Hutt.
Tel: 0800 449 408 Fax: 0800 449 049

NIGERIA: FBFM, Helen Baugh House, 96 St Finbarr's College Road, Akoka, Lagos.
Tel: (01) 7747429/4700218/825775/827264

PHILIPPINES: OMF Literature Inc, 776 Boni Avenue, Mandaluyong City.
Tel: (02) 531 2183 Fax: (02) 531 1960

REPUBLIC OF IRELAND: Scripture Union, 40 Talbot Street, Dublin 1.
Tel: (01) 8363764

SINGAPORE: Campus Crusade Asia Ltd, 315 Outram Road, 06-08 Tan Boon Liat Building,
Singapore 169074. Tel: 222 3640

SOUTH AFRICA: Struik Christian Books, 80 MacKenzie Street, PO Box 1144, Cape Town 8000.
Tel: (021) 462 4360 Fax: (021) 461 3612

SRI LANKA: Christombu Books, 27 Hospital Street, Colombo 1. Tel: (01) 433142/328909

TANZANIA: CLC Christian Book Centre, PO Box 1384, Mkwepu Street, Dar es Salaam.
Tel/Fax: (022) 2119439

USA: CMC Distribution, PO Box 644, Lewiston, New York, 14092-0644. Tel: 1800 325 1297

ZIMBABWE: Word of Life Books, Shop 4, Memorial Building, 35 S Machel Avenue, Harare.
Tel: (04) 781305 Fax: (04) 774739

For e-mail addresses, visit the CWR web site: www.cwr.org.uk

15-Minute Life Changers

An exciting new series offering practical help for trying times. These essential resources for leaders and carers brings together an impressive range of experts who offer biblical help on difficult subjects.

Previously published as the New Perspectives series.

Reducing the Stress Factor
Learn how to deal with stress biblically and effectively.
ISBN: 1-85345-217-3

Facing up to Financial Crisis
Learn how to deal with finances from a biblical perspective.
ISBN: 1-85345-214-9

Living with Long-term Illness
Discover how to also live in the truth that "... in all things God works for the good of those who love him".
ISBN: 1-85345-222-X

Overcoming Redundancy
Face this difficult time by taking the initiative and celebrating your God-given gifts.
ISBN: 1-85345-216-5

A Way out of Despair
Address issues of despair, including suicide, rejection, guilt, self-hate.
ISBN: 1-85345-218-1

Encouraging Carers
This book helps carers to understand that their strength can be found in God.
ISBN: 1-85345-219-X

Building a Better Marriage
A helpful aid for people experiencing a difficult patch, or more serious issues in their marriage.
ISBN: 1-85345-213-0

A Way through Depression
Biblical wisdom to help anyone suffering from this debilitating condition.
ISBN: 1-85345-221-1

Each title presented in a pack of 6 at £5.95
(equivalent to 99p each)